ONE INCH FROM DISASTER

KELLY RANDALL RICKETTS

ONE INCH FROM

True Tales
from the Wilds of
British Columbia

DISASTER

**HARBOUR
PUBLISHING**

Harbour Publishing Co. Ltd.
P.O. Box 219, Madeira Park, BC, VON 2HO
www.harbourpublishing.com

Edited by Pam Robertson
Text design by Carleton Wilson
Cover design by Anna Comfort O'Keeffe
Author photo, back cover, by Ingrid Anne Ricketts
Printed and bound in Canada
Printed on stock made from 100% recycled fibres

Supported by the Province of British Columbia

Harbour acknowledges the support of the Canada Council for the Arts, the Government of Canada, and the Province of British Columbia through the BC Arts Council.

LIBRARY AND ARCHIVES CANADA CATALOGUING IN PUBLICATION

Title: One inch from disaster : true tales from the wilds of British Columbia / Kelly Randall Ricketts.
Names: Ricketts, Kelly Randall, author.
Identifiers: Canadiana (print) 20210372338 | Canadiana (ebook) 20210372419 | ISBN 9781550179262 (softcover) | ISBN 9781550179279 (EPUB)
Subjects: LCSH: Ricketts, Kelly Randall. | LCSH: British Columbia—Biography. | LCSH: Outdoor life—British Columbia. | LCGFT: Autobiographies.
Classification: LCC GV191.52.R53 A3 2022 | DDC 796.5092—dc23

For Ingrid, my children, and God,
who have held me up through the extraordinary journey
that has been my life.

Table of Contents

Acknowledgements   11

Introduction   13

Cry Wolf   15

Devil's Cradle   19

Got Fish?   26

Brotherly Love   30

Dozers and Dynamite   33

Grizzly and Cyclops   36

Rumble at the Dock   42

Dempster Angel   46

Ahhh... Fresh Air and Scary Bear   52

Swim! Swim!   55

That Sinking Feeling   59

The Flying Apple Crate   64

Buried at Sea   69

Golf Balls and Rattlesnakes 73

Once Bitten, Twice Shy 82

Evergreen Warriors 89

Free Wheelin' Three Wheelin' 97

Got a Light? 100

He's Not Dead! 104

Hooked a Beauty! 108

Howe Island Swimming Lesson 113

It's Money All the Same 115

A Lion and a Bear 119

One Load to Go! 127

Missed by an Inch 136

Officer Needs Backup 140

Lights Out 145

Okanagan Idol 1965 152

Jump or Die 157

Post-Game Action 169

Shallow Dive 173

The Code 178

Sucker Punch 184

Once Was More Than Enough 188

Van in Orbit 193

Way Too Close for Comfort 196

Fighting for My Mother's Life 202

A Bear in Hand Is Worth Two in the Bush 209

Man, That's Got to Hurt 213

Miracle Baby 220

Random Act 225

Hobbles and Horses 228

Just Fall 236

Lights, Camera, Action! 248

About the Author 253

Acknowledgements

At first I hesitated in writing an acknowledgements section for these stories from my life. Some of the characters I've included were the source of great sorrow, anger and feelings of abandonment. Many years ago I learned to forgive both others and myself, and this opened up my road to healing. Now I can remember the good things I learned over these many years— each was trying to teach me a critical life lesson, on purpose or simply by chance.

I am indebted to my mother Rose, who taught me how to work and to work hard, raising eight children by herself, working two full-time jobs to do that and showing me what commitment means. My father Bruce, for all his faults, would never allow "I can't" or "it's impossible" to be part of my vocabulary, but instead drummed into me that I had to keep trying and not give up (unfortunately, he would not take his own advice and try to keep his marriage together with my mom). His method of hands-off teaching instilled in me an attentive and focused approached to learning, helping me to develop the ability to problem solve at a young age.

I married my second wife, Ingrid, thirty-three years ago. I am deeply grateful to Ingrid for being my friend, my soulmate, my champion and more, much more to me than I dreamed was possible. She is the first and only woman I have ever truly loved in my life, in the way you can love only that one special companion. Thank you, Ingrid, for taking a chance on a long shot, for believing in me and for helping me to become a far better version of myself than I was before you came into my life.

My nine children have filled my life with every emotion conceivable and helped me to grow in ways I could never have imagined. Fatherhood has been one heck of a ride, with its share of lows—including burying my son Brent when he was only fourteen—but far more highs. For the forty-seven years I have been raising them, my children have given me countless blessings.

Thank you to all my friends who encouraged me to write my stories for others to read.

Most of all, I want to thank my Heavenly Father, who has borne me up through some very difficult times and countless heartaches. Who has never given up on me, even when I had all but given up on myself, especially in my early years. And who has saved my life or delivered me from serious bodily harm many a time, some of which you will read about in these pages.

Introduction

This collection is inspired by real events that have happened in my life, with the stories evolving out of ones I told my children over the years. While they were growing up, we had a long-standing storytelling custom that we called The Club. From the time they were very young, I would regularly gather all the kids together onto our large master bed and turn off the lights, at which point the bed transformed and took us on a journey into the unknown. Sometimes the bed magically changed into a hot-air balloon floating over majestic vistas, or a pirate ship sailing the oceans in search of vast treasures and ill-gotten booty, with us plundering wherever we wanted— whatever the children could imagine, or I could. When that adventure came to its finish, we would all settle in for a story from my life.

The children looked forward to The Club so much that they were still coming in to take part when they were in their early teens. Now, with the kids all gone on to their own life pursuits, I wanted to write about my experiences, both the good and not so good, in hopes they might more fully understand where I came from and what shaped me into who I became and who I am today.

Many of the stories in this book were never told to the children in full—they were, at least in my opinion, too young to hear some of the more graphic details. In fact, even some adults may find them difficult to read. But the truth needs to be told, unsullied and in its rawest form, to be able to convey the feelings I had: the anger and the humour, and even the sorrow.

In these pages you will find stories about happy days, near tragedy, rage, pain and some truly unbelievable experiences, with a few that even touch on the supernatural. Because these events happened over the past six decades, it is possible I may have some of the characters' names wrong, and timelines could be off by a small margin, but the actual circumstances and events themselves were vivid enough to hold my recollections firm. I hope my stories will bring you entertainment and enlightenment, and possibly even a sense of confederacy on things you too may have experienced or survived.

Cry Wolf

As a young man and an avid hunter, I took advantage of as many opportunities to hunt as the regulations would allow. Archery season was one of those opportunities. It afforded me the chance to be out ahead of the many hunters who chose to wait until the opening of the main firearms season. This early bow season gave me as much as a two-week advantage. The game would be less wary: no guns of autumn had yet been heard to provide a forewarning to the deer and bear populations.

The archery season's opening day on Vancouver Island, where I was living in my early hunting years, was normally in the latter part of August. It would be warm, for sure. The days were long but a long day in the field hunting was always better than any day not hunting, or doing anything else for that matter. This story takes place up near Adam River, about a sixty-kilometre drive north of Sayward. We considered Sayward to be the start of the North Island region.

Most bow hunters would be out combing the timber and open slash for deer or bear on weekends. But the logging company that held the timber forest licence for the area was not currently logging the location I had chosen to hunt. I had a couple of weekdays off from work so, to gain even more advantage, I simply went out on a weekday. It worked out that a buddy, Bob, who had accompanied me on many hunts and fishing trips over the years, was able to join me.

We arrived at our chosen location. Two areas appeared to hold the best chance for success, or at least a good chance to spot game and get in a stalk. As we came to a crossroads, I decided I would carry on by foot, travelling up the road we were on until I reached the next logged area. Bob would take the right fork and drive a kilometre or two up to another area to the east where we had spotted some nice bucks in our pre-season scouting.

With the sun still not making its appearance but the skies starting to brighten in the advent of its rising, we parted company. The first couple of hundred metres along the road brought me into a timbered area. The large coastal timber created a cathedral-like entrance with darkness and limited visibility, even as the sun was starting to chase the early-morning shadows away. The air was cool and crisp with the fresh smell of moss and the spruce that towered along the road on either side.

As I rounded a corner, without warning two wolves materialized. Standing in the middle of the road, they looked upon me with intent. I stopped in my tracks, caught off guard by their sudden appearance. I should not have been so surprised, though. I knew the wolf problem on the Island was becoming a serious one, yet to date I had seen only a few. We were at a Mexican standoff.

The wolves seemed content to stay in the middle of the road, watching me with focused stares. I was standing somewhat frozen, in a transfixed state. As I looked at my fifty-five-pound Ben Pearson Recurve and my pointed sticks, they did not give me a lot of reassurance. How I wished I was holding my trusty .30-06.

For some unknown and foolish reason, I carried on toward the wolves, maybe because they didn't look as big as the wolves I had seen in the past. They might have been just a couple of wandering juveniles. Or maybe I felt I could dominate them, if push came to shove, with my Robin Hood–like prowess with my bow. That, coupled with ignorance and a lack of common sense to go the other way, kept me moving forward.

I followed the two along the dark stretch of timbered roadside, thinking I might even get close enough for a shot. They seemed to be content to let me follow them, always staying about thirty-five metres ahead of me, which was out of my range. I hunted bare bow, no sights or fancy equipment, just my instinct, and my instinct said twenty metres maximum range.

I was dressed in camouflage and was wearing a liberal quantity of deer-cover scent. They might not have known I was Man, the Alpha Hunter. With them seemingly showing no fear of me, on we went. If I lagged behind a little too much they would stop, turn and wait until I was once again within that thirty-five metres or so. Once I was in that intangible range, off they would go again, walking as purposefully as before.

As we rounded another corner I could see that, nearly a hundred and fifty metres ahead, the dark, timbered roadway opened into a logging slash. Suddenly the two young wolves vanished, rushing into the dark forest around me. In that instant, all hell broke loose.

The silence of our fifteen-minute walking vigil was broken with growling, snarling and all manner of frightful, bone-chilling sounds. I could identify the growls of older members of the pack as well as the whining yips of young subordinate pups. They reverberated on both sides of me. It became clear that I had been led into a trap!

Fear struck me frozen and voiceless. Any moment I expected to see the timber release the pack of demons with slashing fangs ready to rip and tear the flesh from my still-living carcass. The terror I felt, in an instant, turned to anger mixed with fear. I screamed at the unseen horde, "Come and get me! I'll kill you all!"

Then, with no warning, and as if on command, there was silence again. Only the beating of my pounding heart and my quick, laboured breaths could be heard. I once again stood frozen, still anticipating an attack, in the calm before the storm. I never moved a muscle but stayed transfixed on the timber on both sides of me for what seemed like an eternity. Reason finally overwhelmed shock and fear, telling me that as quick as they had come they had gone.

A few hours later, Bob arrived to pick me up. He was not surprised to hear about my earlier encounter, as he had seen no deer, but ample signs of wolf activity.

Later that fall, I was talking to one of the local conservation officers. He told me that a huge pack had been identified in that very area, counted to be nearly forty wolves. An extremely large pack by any standards. Suffice it to say, the next time I hunted in the Adam River area I was packing heat!

Devil's Cradle

For months Kim and I had been planning to go to the Nahwitti River at the north end of Vancouver Island. Kim was my cousin and a very good friend, almost more like a brother. We shared many outdoor adventures over the years, and this one was by far the most memorable. We hoped to experience what could be an incredible four days of steelhead fishing, unsurpassed even by what you'd find on some of the most famous steelhead rivers in the world, such as the mighty Dean River, situated at the head of the channel it is named for on the mainland of BC, or the remarkable Gold River, closer to home on Vancouver Island. But for this trip, the Nahwitti was our destination.

The Nahwitti River was in a remote Island location with no roads or access trails. We were confident that we would be the first people in recent history to actually fish some of the spectacular pools that we knew the river contained. It was May 1974. We had no Google Earth or GPS to guide our way or provide clear imagery, so we didn't know what to expect. It would truly be an adventure in discovery. I couldn't wait.

At 5:00 a.m. Saturday, we finished packing all the necessary gear, then checked it twice, even three times, before kissing our families goodbye and pulling out of my driveway.

We travelled north toward Port Hardy via the Gold River Highway, turning onto a gravel road just northeast of Gold River.

At the time, that was the way to Port Hardy, near the northern part of Vancouver Island. The Island Highway would not be constructed along the North Island route for at least a decade.

We choked on the dust of many kilometres of washboard gravel road until we reached Port Hardy. Considering the fact that we were only into late May, the heat was quite stifling. However it did not lessen our growing anticipation and excitement. Soon Kim and I would be hiking into the wild and untouched Nahwitti area.

We had our last restaurant meal in Port Hardy, then made the final sixty-five-kilometre drive to the end of a logging road. This would be our starting point. At 9:00 a.m., with packs loaded, after another final check to make absolutely sure we had everything, we were good to go. The going was slow as we descended a steep hill not far from where we had parked at the end of the road.

The plan was simple: follow the Nahwitti River, fishing our way down until we reached its final destination, the ocean. The plan only partially worked, however, as we encountered windfalls and the biggest obstacle of all, the much loathed devil's bush.

It was a thick, thorny hell that taxed one's resolve and patience to the extreme. The closer we tried to stay to the river, the worse the devil's bush was. Hacking our way through, metre by metre, with me wielding my machete like a seasoned jungle fighter, we soon put some distance behind us. With nine-plus kilometres to go, it would most likely take the rest of the day to reach the mouth of the Nahwitti.

Along the way, we were able to find a couple of good pools where we could take a much-needed break from our bushwhacking trials. Taking out the rods, we tried some fishing. After a couple of attempts, we managed only one good hit, so we soldiered on. Late into the afternoon, we were still hacking our way through the maze of downed trees and the ever-expanding jungle of devil's bush.

Suddenly we broke through into a cleared opening, a perfect circle about nine metres in diameter. There was not a twig, leaf or blade of grass; only soft cool dirt beneath our feet, as if it had been groomed by some meticulous groundskeeper. Placed exactly in the middle of this strange and mysterious clearing was a baby's cradle made from small interlocking branches.

The cradle was the size and shape of an apple box. As Kim and I gazed upon this fascinating object, we stayed silent, coming to our own conclusions about its existence and purpose. As we silently pondered its meaning, we could not help feeling uneasy, as though there were something present that we could not see with the naked eye but could feel within our very being.

Studying the circle further, we noticed there were no footprints or signs of any life, not even birds or squirrels, which were usually plentiful. Something should have been etched across this earthen canvas. No trails were found leading in, yet something or someone had maintained this place, placed a baby's cradle in it, and even guarded it from any intrusion, at least until we stumbled onto it.

Without saying a word, we left the ominous clearing and continued on.

After two more hard-fought hours, we came to a wide spot on the river and cooled our feet. In fact we could hear the surf as it crashed on the beach, likely no more than a few kilometres away.

We talked about the possibility of just carrying on to the beach, but sheer exhaustion and hunger persuaded us otherwise. After a nutritious meal of macaroni and cheese, we would need a good night's sleep, so camping for the night was in order.

Following our feast, and after setting up our tent, I decided to read until we crashed for the evening and went inside the tent. Lying on my sleeping bag, half asleep, I was jolted back to full consciousness when Kim rushed in.

With a fearful look in his eyes and terror in his voice, he said, "We need to leave right now!"

"What are you talking about?" I complained. "We just got here and I'm beat."

"We need to leave, and leave now!" he exclaimed again with even more conviction in his voice.

Reluctantly, I acquiesced to his request, or rather his demand. Kim wasn't one to elaborate much on anything, so I didn't bother pressing him for the reason for his sudden order. Maybe deep down, I actually felt the same way he did.

Kim was hurriedly stuffing his belongings back into his pack, so I worked at breaking camp. Without any further discussion, we shouldered our packs and began the arduous trek back up the river. With only about an hour and a half of daylight left, time was of the essence.

We followed our freshly broken trail back until it became too difficult to see. The rapidly increasing darkness began to enshroud us. The river ran slowly and quietly. Whenever we tried to move away from it to avoid the tangle of windfalls and thick bush, we became disoriented in the dark and would lose our way. Fearing we would end up hopelessly lost, we realized the only alternative was to travel *in* the river, or at least in the river as much as it would allow.

As we travelled into the night, a not quite full moon overhead silhouetted the trees on either side of the river. I began to feel very uneasy, and I sensed this in Kim too. It wasn't the travelling through the bush in the dark, for we had done so many times (even in country teeming with bear and cougar). No, this was a sense of anxiety we had never felt before. We stumbled along in the dark, waist-deep in water sometimes only a metre from the undercut banks. We sensed we were being watched from the dark that surrounded us.

Judging by the way the river was making a turn to the west, we knew that we were close to *the place*, the place of the cradle. Almost as soon as I realized that, I began to hear things. First just a twig snap, then the shuffle of a foot. Then I thought I could make out movement in the brush paralleling the river. The feeling of being observed became even stronger. At times I would stop breathing in order to hear any sound or a warning that my breaths would obscure.

Suddenly Kim collapsed in front of me, completely going under the water. As he rose back to the surface I grabbed him by the pack, which was now completely saturated. His old-style cotton-filled sleeping bag probably weighed thirteen kilograms alone. Nearing total exhaustion, Kim told me I would need to carry his pack. When I protested, as I too was facing total exhaustion, he replied, "You're bigger and stronger. You need to carry my sleeping bag at least." I reluctantly agreed.

My legs began to stiffen up, the result of cold water and the still-present sense of foreboding. Finally we broke through at the point we had climbed down to the river, nearly twenty hours earlier. Dragging our sorry and spent bodies up the hill and over the remaining two hundred metres to the truck took all we had. We threw the packs in the box of the truck with our fishing gear.

Still soaked from the river, and the promise of a new day still an hour away, we slumped into the seat of the truck and slept. I don't think we moved at all until the stifling heat of the sun, radiating through the truck windows, brought us groggily to our senses.

As the years—in fact the decades—passed by, the truth of what Kim had witnessed and felt that night was never known. Finally in April of 2016, shortly before his passing, Kim finally revealed to me why he had so adamantly demanded we leave that place that night.

From the moment we'd come upon that cradle in the mysterious circle, Kim had felt a presence watching us. When we stopped for the night and while I read in the tent, he had felt a darkness approach him. A cold, maleficent entity overwhelmed him with fear, and with the knowledge that some evil design was in the making for us if we did not leave immediately.

As Kim recounted that evening to me those many decades later, his voice was intense with emotion. I may never know the significance of that mysterious clearing or of the cradle that was placed precisely in the middle of it. I have at times felt the urge to retrace our steps and try to find some remnant of its existence. However, two significant factors have persuaded me not to pursue it. First, the chance of it still being there after almost half a century is not highly likely, and second, the chance of it still being there after this many years *is* highly likely!

Got Fish?

We had just moved to Kelowna. It was 1964 and my parents had bought a house up on DeHart Road in the South Kelowna area. I'm not sure why we moved, but I missed Campbell River and my friends. Dad never really moved with us—he only made a few brief appearances—and for the most part it was only Mom and us kids from that time on. I enrolled in the elementary school that was only about a kilometre away. It was a little difficult starting in a new school after only one month in the classroom in Campbell River, but the teacher I would have—the stunning redhead Miss Gerlinger—made anything I had to do worth it. But that's another story.

School went okay. Fall turned into winter, then spring came early that year. I had always loved fishing, but my teenaged brothers never really fished and my dad had left the family so I had no one to take me. I would hear about kids going out with their dads and catching nice big rainbows and kokanee and long to be in their place. Generally, most kids ignored me, especially because of my stuttering. I felt stupid and abandoned, and found my best friend, at least at that early stage of my life, to be me. Much of the time I played alone and certainly didn't get asked to go fishing with anyone. Besides, I was still the new kid.

One beautiful April afternoon on my way home from school, I was wandering along the road in a bit of a daydream. I was surprised out of my reverie by what sounded like splashing. It hadn't rained for at least a week or more. There were no puddles and certainly no lakes or ponds anywhere, yet I heard something splashing. Nah, I must have been imagining it. Not hearing anything more, I continued on my way.

There it was again. *Splash! Splash!* Okay, I knew I heard splashing now but the question was, from where? At this point I was near the junction of DeHart Road, where we lived, and another that led to the school I had just left. I stood on the edge of the road, straining to hear the splashing again, prepared this time to pinpoint its source.

There it was again, but this time I heard and *saw* the splashing. Running parallel to the road that went north toward my school was a metal irrigation flume that provided water for the orchards. At least, that's what I believe they were used for. I ran to the edge of the flume where I had seen the splash. Climbing up on a metal rail, I could look into the flume. It entered a concrete pipe that ran under DeHart Road then resurfaced on the other side to continue on down alongside the road. In a metal grate that kept large debris such as branches from plugging up the flume, I could not believe what I saw!

There, with its enormous head stuck halfway through the grate, was the biggest rainbow trout I had ever seen or even thought existed. It flailed in the grating, unable to back out or go forward. I was a little fearful of grabbing this Moby-Dick of the trout world, but desire overcame fear.

I reached in and grabbed the monster fish by the fork of the tail. I was barely able to get my hands fully around it but then, shoving the fingers of my right hand into the gill plate and grabbing its bottom jaw cartilage, I jerked hard backwards. The fish came out and made a dramatic flip, freeing itself from my hands, but fortunately it landed on the ground right beside me. I pounced on it! Finding a rock the size of an orange by the ditch, I dispatched the behemoth. This remarkable fish was bigger than any of the fish other kids bragged about from their fishing trips.

I beamed with exultation. I'd caught the biggest rainbow ever and done it with my bare hands. After slaying the fish, I rinsed off the gravel that marred his impressive body. I couldn't wait to show my mother. She would be so proud of me. I ran as fast as I could, carrying my school books and my huge fish.

Arriving home, I laid the trout on our garage floor then went in to tell my mom. I knew she wouldn't be happy if I brought the fish into the house before it was cleaned.

Actually, I kind of didn't know how to clean a fish anyway. I opened the door, hollering to my mom to come quick and see what I'd done. Now, the normal response to "Come quick and see what I did!" in our family would have been, "Now what did you break/mutilate/lose or get into trouble about?"

As she came to the back door, I grabbed her hand and told her to follow me. She was still protesting, "What are you doing?" When she entered the garage, her first words were "Where did you get that?" in a mother's accusing tone. I assured her I had not stolen it from anywhere, but that I'd caught it with my bare hands out of the flume just down the road.

I don't think she ever really believed me, but she was not about to turn down a big, beautiful and very delicious rainbow trout. She helped me clean the fish, and later that day, our whole family enjoyed a fantastic meal—one I had caught with my bare hands!

Brotherly Love

Growing up in the Ricketts home, we felt it was important to be able to defend ourselves from any kind of attack. I never had any desire to be a fighter as a child, but having violence thrust into my life and facing some sort of it fairly regularly, it only seemed reasonable that I might become a competitive fighter, and the training would come in handy. Later in life it would be inevitable, as a release from years of built-up anger and frustration.

Fighting was a way of life in our family, even including my mother, Rose. I personally witnessed at least forty fights before I turned fourteen and left home to find my own way. My oldest brother, Robin, had been shot at and was involved in fights that included all kinds of weapons. I myself was involved in three or four fights, that I can remember, where a weapon was used.

My brother Terry, who was three years older than me, loved to fight. Before his death in June of 2014 at age sixty-two, Terry probably had over two hundred street fights in his life. Not wrestling matches, but serious fights that would often require a visit to the Emergency unit for the losing party. It wasn't often Terry, but he had his share of hospital visits too. Terry was five-foot-five and weighed sixty-six kilograms, but many times he took on guys almost a foot taller and up to fifty kilos heavier.

He was also a world-class gymnast. I admired him more than all my other siblings.

Let's back up to the fall of 1968, when I had just turned thirteen years old. When I arrived home from school one afternoon, Terry met me at the front entrance of our home. He handed me a small bath towel and instructed me to wrap it around my left forearm and grab the remaining end of the towel in my left hand. I refused, questioning why. With impatience in his voice, he again ordered me to "Just do it!"

Not wanting to anger him, I followed his command and wrapped the towel around my arm as instructed. Once I had wrapped my arm, he drew a butcher knife from behind his back with a blade about twenty centimetres long and razor sharp. Mom worked in a butcher shop and her knives were kept very sharp.

He lunged at me. I jumped back and bumped into the front door. Terry yelled for me to use the wrapped arm as a shield, just as a jacket or sweater could be used. I was petrified and feared for my life. Whether I did what he said or didn't, either way I did not see this ending well.

Terry backed away and urged me forward. I took a couple fearful steps forward, then he lunged at me again, using a straight jab with the knife at my midsection. I instinctively brushed my hand down to deflect the knife. It stuck into the towel that guarded me for the moment. Terry pulled back the knife, then said, "Good! Just like that. Now I'll do it again. This time try and grab my knife hand with your free hand after you block it with your protected arm."

I protested again, shaking in fear. He assured me it would work. "If you don't want to get shivved then you're going to have to learn." Terry made four or five more attempts. I half dodged and half blocked the last few attempts and with luck was able, on one occasion, to grab his knife hand.

Thinking I was now well versed in defending and protecting myself from a deadly knife attack, Terry called it quits and told me I'd done well. He was either lying to me or was a hell of a lot more convinced of that than I was, or would ever be. I can't say that my subsequent success at street fighting or in the ring was because of those early self-defence classes, but who knows? I have only lost one fight on the street—but I lost that one good!

Aww, there is nothing like brotherly love.

Dozers and Dynamite

There comes a time in your life when the stars are aligned in your favour perfectly and you need to immediately go out and buy a lottery ticket. Your luck is so beyond good that it defies all reasonable description or understanding. Let me qualify this statement by saying I don't gamble, nor would I ever encourage it in anyone's life. However, if I had bought a lottery ticket back in April of 1982, I would not have considered it gambling. It would have been an absolute fact that I would have won.

The morning out at Kyuquot Bay, situated on the west coast of Vancouver Island, started exactly the same way that each day of the past week or so had started. It was a beautiful spring sky in radiant blue, fresh sea air filled my lungs and warm westerly breezes blew in from far out on the Pacific Ocean.

I was employed by a road-building company out of Delta. My job as a swamper on the track drill involved driving the truck and dozer and being kind of a utility man or jack-of-all-trades. I did some welding as well. The day before, Brian, the rock drill operator, and I had prepared a cut in the side of the mountain at the end of the road we were building. We were going to drill and blast a vertical face for our quarry. It was to be used for the gravel and fractured rock needed to finish the rough subgrade we had just pioneered.

We had not started to drill the quarry at that point, but we had cleared the site. The next job would be to walk up the track drill and drill the face. Brian was farther down the grade, drilling off some ditch line. We would be blasting that later in the week. I drove the 4×4 truck up to the site to do a final check. I wanted to be assured that when Brian arrived to begin drilling in a couple of hours, the site would indeed be prepped and ready.

Seeing a couple of areas that needed to be levelled a bit more, I decided to fire up the D6 dozer that was parked at the drilling site. I wanted to improve some of the lumpy spots. I warmed up the D6, then began to grade the site, running back and forth levelling the rough spots, almost by instinct. As it was me who had built the drilling site earlier in the week, I never looked behind. I knew, without any concern, where I was because of my previous track imprints.

After nearly completely clearing the area, I worked my way to the seaward side of the road. I decided to back the dozer down the road a bit farther away from where it was parked originally. That way I would not have to move it when Brian arrived with the drill. The earth below me was ablaze with sparks as the steel tracks ground into the hard West Coast granite.

I kept going backwards until suddenly the D6 started to climb steeply behind me. Thinking I had walked the dozer up onto a large rock that might have been dislodged from the road bed, I kept backing up. To my complete horror, I noticed a large blue tarp underneath the right track. I could see it was torn in places, which exposed what it was covering. I could barely breathe. I began to shake and broke out into a cold sweat as I became fully conscious of what I had just done.

I was sitting on twenty-five cases of Powerfrac dynamite—twenty-four sticks and eighteen kilograms per case. I was sitting in a dangerous, precarious position on over 450 kilograms of very destructive explosives. Some might argue that it would need a detonation of some sort for it to explode. However, I'd been taught that an open flame or sparks could ignite exposed dynamite. On the hard granite, I could see shredded cases and huge sticks of dynamite strewn beneath the track.

Nearly frozen in fear, I sat helplessly trying to decide what I should do next. Those thoughts were coupled with the anger I felt at myself for doing such an absolutely stupid and thoughtless thing. It made it even more painful and humiliating to know it was me who, only the day before, had hauled all that dynamite up to the site. I was the one who had covered it with the very tarp that was now shredded below me.

I sat motionless for many long minutes, anchored by fear, too scared to make any move. Then it happened. Abruptly, without any conscious thought, I placed the shifter of the D6 into forward gear. I began to walk the dozer back off that mutilated mountain of sheer, instant destruction. It was as though I was oblivious to any possible consequence.

By some divine intervention, or pure dumb luck, I was able to walk the D6 clear of the dynamite. My exhale and subsequent "Thank you, God" was probably heard fifty kilometres away.

As I said earlier, I should have immediately gone and bought a lottery ticket. It would have been an absolutely guaranteed win, at least on that day!

Grizzly and Cyclops

Kimsquit, near the head of Dean Channel in the Kitimat Ranges of the Coast Mountains, is probably one of the most exciting and picturesque locations in beautiful British Columbia that I have ever seen. Massive, craggy mountains hold snow all year, then release thunderous avalanches throughout the early spring and summer. While I was working for Mayo Lumber at Kimsquit, one such avalanche came within forty metres of our camp. Stories were told of an avalanche that was so large it completely destroyed the camp a few years earlier. Yet they rebuilt it in the same spot…

The world-renowned Dean River, with its beautiful scenery and wildlife in abundance (especially grizzly bears), offered some of the most spectacular river fishing you'll ever find. The salmon fishing was awesome, whether from the log dump on shore or out in the channel. Steelhead trout reached weights of ten-plus kilograms. They were so plentiful that they provided enough explosive action to wear out even the most seasoned and fit fisherman.

One of my buddies who worked in the shop with me, Rick, had looked forward to accompanying me on such a fishing expedition. I wanted to prove to him that the mighty Dean River's reputation was more than just hype. With two other fellows, I had already fished the Dean earlier in the month and had great success, landing two beautiful steelhead, four and eight kilos respectively. As luck would have it, one day soon after that Rick and I were able to finish at 4:30 p.m., a rare occurrence as we usually worked overtime. We grabbed our gear, borrowed one of the company pickups and got ready to drive out to Seventeen Mile.

After loading the truck with our fishing gear and two pieces of pie from the cookhouse for later, we headed out and soon arrived at our site. The fishing was slow, as the water had risen from some heavy rains and snow melt. The water had become quite turbid, which can affect the fishing dramatically. We had a couple of bumps, but no fish.

While we were fishing, a large, lone grizzly lumbered onto the bank on the opposite shore. It wandered along the shore parallel to Rick and me, looking somewhat bemused at our presence, but never venturing forth as if to cross. We reeled in our lines and prepared to vamoose if the bear decided to take a closer look. Fortunately, it turned back into the bush and vanished.

Rick and I fished for another fifteen minutes or so with no bites. We decided it was time to head back to camp as it was getting late. When we returned to the truck we noticed, with some dismay, that the passenger's-side front tire was almost flat. We looked for a jack, only to discover we didn't have one. We hoped the tire would hold enough air to get us the twenty-seven kilometres back to camp.

We pulled onto the main logging road and hurried along. Unfortunately, the tire only lasted for about five more kilometres before going completely flat. By this time the approaching darkness was evidence that we would be very late getting back to camp. Driving at a snail's pace with the flat tire, we approached the crossing of Skuce Creek and the Dean River at the Mile Twelve marker. Then I remembered something.

There was a track drill parked on a pull-off just past the bridge. I pulled the truck into the landing, hoping to find a jack to change the flat. The tire now resembled a shredded mess of rubber and steel cord. We grabbed our flashlight and hurried to the drill, only to find out that it too had no jack! We had a wheel wrench but no jack. What idiot would take the jack out of the truck in the first place? Dang!

By this time we were getting hungry and tired. My watch said it was just after 10:30 p.m. The pieces of apple pie were long gone and my stomach growled for more. Returning to the truck to commiserate and complain with Rick, a new thought came to me. If we could drive the truck up onto the bank on the sloping hillside in front of us, we could maybe dig the gravel out from under the flat tire, suspending it. The truck would be high-centred on the bank. Then we could pull the tire off and change it, then drag ourselves back off the slope in four-wheel drive and be on our way. Rick and I agreed that could work.

I ran the truck up onto the bank and, using a shovel I found in the track drill, dug out the wheel. The truck gradually lowered until the front end came to rest on the slope, finally freeing the tire enough for us to pull it off and change it. Rick grabbed the wheel wrench from behind the seat and I used the flashlight to give him light while he removed the lug nuts. As he was taking off the last one, however, we heard a woofing kind of sound, like a throaty cough, then noticed rocks rolling down the gravel bank in front of us.

The bank rose to about twelve metres high, at which point it was enveloped by the dark timber above. We froze, straining to hear if any more noise was forthcoming. Nothing unusual, but the still of the dark night and its eerie silence was both heard and felt. We removed the tire, placed on our spare and Rick tightened the wheel nuts back on. When he had only three left to put on, we heard another distinctive, deep-throated cough, and rocks came rolling down again.

The rocks were being dislodged by something moving on the edge where the timber and open hillside merged. The gravel and small rocks were rolling down the hill in a consistent pattern—left to right then back right to left. We both knew what we were hearing and witnessing. We had the unwanted attention of a bear, more than likely a grizzly. There were plenty of them in the area.

Frantically, we jumped into the truck and slammed the doors. Sitting motionless with the truck running, neither of us said a word. We only stared, transfixed, up the hill in front of us. It was obvious we were going to be there all night, or until our visitor came down to acquaint itself with us.

Neither scenario was a viable option. We agreed that we would jump out on three. I would shine the light up at the top of the bank near the timberline, watch for our unwanted observer and keep him preoccupied. Rick would quickly tighten the last three lug nuts. I counted *1 – 2 – 3 – GO!* Rick's door didn't open. I emphasized with a bit more emotion that we needed to finish getting the tire on—and *right now!*—or we wouldn't be going anywhere.

Gravel kept tumbling down in that same pattern, back and forth, as if the bear was trying to decide its next move. It seemed intent on watching us below, though, and reluctant to leave. With the truck running and in four-wheel, ready to go, I counted to three again. This time we both jumped out and Rick went to work like a first-class NASCAR pit crewman with me standing vigil beside him, continuing to shine the light up the hill.

While Rick was screwing on the last nut, we heard not only the deep-throated cough as before, but a low, menacing growl that sounded like it was coming from a beast of epic proportions. A large slide of gravel began to careen down the hill. Unable to see much of anything now as the flashlight batteries were getting weak, I dove over the hood of the truck and jumped in. Rick was already in and screaming to get the hell out of there. I slammed the truck into reverse and turned to look out the back window. To my horror I could see a single glowing eye approaching us from behind the truck—and it was clearly not a bear's. Rick, also turning to look back, yelled, "What the f— is that?"

I continued to reverse, unable to get off the hill, where we were still anchored. With an angry bear in the front and this one-eyed apparition coming even closer to the rear of us, I rocked the truck madly back and forth. Rick, the whole time, was screaming, "Get this f—ing truck out of here! What the f— is that thing?" over and over. "I don't know," I said, "but I'm backing over it."

At last the wheels all fully engaged and we were able to get free of the hill. I jammed the truck into gear and left a trail of rocks and gravel flying in the path behind me. Both of us were still shaken up quite badly, in total disbelief of what had just happened. What the hell was that one-eyed thing we had seen through the back window? We carried on toward camp with heart rates slowly returning to normal.

As we rounded a corner on the road, we noticed another vehicle approaching us. As it came closer, I noticed it had only one headlight. Could that have been what we'd witnessed? I knew it wasn't only my frightened and vivid imagination because Rick had seen the same thing. But we could never be sure. The one thing for sure was that Rick and I were two scared dudes. We were not soon to forget the night of the grizzly and the Cyclops on the Dean.

Rumble at the Dock

They say that all of the greatest stories, shared across kitchen tables or around campfires, always start with truth—to some degree. Some more, some less. They are usually, at the very least, exciting and colourful. This story tells the Truth, as well as memory will allow.

It had been a beautiful late June Saturday in Kelowna, located in the middle of the scenic Okanagan region of BC. The day was slowly giving way to evening. My buddy Colin and I decided we would head over to the old *Fintry Queen* ferry dock on the west side of Okanagan Lake. We had heard that my older brother Terry and his buddies were having a big party. The ferry dock was a popular hangout for partiers, usually teenagers and young adults, and Terry and his friends were regulars.

Colin and I hitchhiked over to the Westside, getting a ride fairly quickly, as was the norm back in those days. People back then seemed far more trusting and willing to give fourteen-year-olds a lift.

We arrived at the ferry dock's parking area just as darkness was setting in. Indeed, a huge party was well underway. Cars were parked everywhere you could find a place to squeeze in a vehicle. Even by my brother's party standards, it was huge. Colin and I walked between the rows of cars, heading to the ferry dock. That was where the tough guys, or at least the dominant guys, would take up office.

As we passed a big Chev on our left, some guy stuck his head out the rear window and told me to "F— off." Without hesitation, I fired a right hand into the dude's face. It erupted in a bloody mess. Unfazed, we carried on—after all, this was my brother's party. Who was going to mess with me for hitting that goof?

Near the end of the parking area we could see the landing for the dock. As we strained to find Terry in among the sixteen or more guys who were there, we heard people behind us yelling, "There he is! That's the guy right over there!" We were not sure who they were referring to, and we kept walking. Eventually we jumped up onto the steel loading ramp, but we were still unable to see Terry anywhere.

Suddenly someone started yelling threats that were definitely aimed at me. As the guy got closer, he steadily issued threats of bodily harm to me, to which I replied, "Anytime, a—hole." Even though this dude was probably seventeen or eighteen, I was not too concerned. Not because I thought I was such a badass, but I really believed that at any moment Terry would show up and tell these guys that I was his younger brother. If they touched me, they would pay dearly for so doing. The Ricketts family stuck together when it came to each other's well-being, at least physically.

The guy then rushed me. I sidestepped his rush and caught him with a right hand, and he hit the metal safety railing that lined the side of the ramp. As he hit the rail he lost his balance and almost fell over. Seeing a possible advantage, I spun around, grabbed his jacket and belt and helped him continue his momentum over the side. I gripped his jacket as he hung there. Girls screaming, guys yelling—it was a very tense situation.

As long as I was holding this guy by the jacket and belt, preventing him from falling on the rocks below, I felt I had some control of the situation, even as some other guys came closer. I still held the trump card, literally, in my hands. With Colin standing by my side, at four-foot-eleven and barely more than a buck ten, I knew he was not going to be much help when and if they were going to rush me all at once.

One of the bigger guys started to make threats, identifying himself as the brother of the guy I was holding by the jacket. I challenged him to make his move, but told him I would have to drop his brother to accommodate him. That worked; he stopped his advance and threats. The whole time this was happening, the kid who was hanging by his jacket was pleading, "Don't drop me, man, please don't drop me."

The sounds of girls' screams were now muffled by the sounds of cars. As they screeched out of the ferry dock's parking area we could hear shouts of "That guy is f—ing crazy." At this point only about three or four of the group were left on the ramp, including the brother of the guy I was still holding.

My arm was weakening to the point of being unable to hold him much longer, though. His tenuous grip on one of the rail supports was not helping me much to support his weight. The older brother was no longer yelling threats at me, but was now pleading with me not to drop his brother. Reaching around with both hands, I pulled him back up onto the dock ramp.

Once he was able to get to his feet, I faced what I believed was a forthcoming beating. I no longer held the upper hand. Instead, these last few guys ran to their vehicle and sped away, leaving me and Colin standing alone in the now quiet of the summer night. With only the gentle splashing of water on the beach, we started on the hour-long walk back to Kelowna, still having found no sign of my brother.

A couple of months later, while I was talking with Terry, this event came up in our conversation. Terry, pointing his finger at me in an accusing but amused way, exclaimed, "You! You were the one!" I must have had a bewildered look on my face, so he went on to explain.

The RCMP had pulled him into the station to question him about the big brawl that he and his gang were involved in out at the ferry dock in June. It was easy to believe it was a Ricketts who had perpetrated it, if that was what people were saying, as fighting was a big part of our family life—and being poor and angry I'm sure had a lot to do with it. Apparently, the police had accused Terry and his gang of chasing off three-hundred-and-change grad partiers from Penticton. Yes, the notorious Ricketts gang of two had struck again!

Dempster Angel

I believe that at least once in everyone's experience, you meet someone who has a significant impact or influence on your life.

I was married at a very young age, at a post-pubescent sixteen, and soon found myself resentful of my much senior wife of twenty-five, Lynne, who had two children from a previous relationship. Although I had been on my own for nearly two years, was working full-time and considered myself to be a very responsible young man, I'd made a huge mistake. That mistake had brought me to this place, where I was now a husband and father. I never really loved my first wife of six years, but I stayed loyal and provided for my family the best that I could.

Four years after we got together, I acquired a job working for Majestic Pipeliners on the Dempster Highway in the Yukon, which was being constructed to Inuvik. I worked there for about two months as a welder. I enjoyed my job and the money was awesome, with me earning $6,000 a month. That was a lot of money back in 1977. Lynne was at home in Campbell River with our children, Brent, Wade and Kelly Jr.

One afternoon I needed to get something from my room at lunchtime. Heading over to the complex of trailers, I came in the north door and crossed through the hallway that ran through the middle of the cross-shaped layout of units. As I reached the far south end of the hall where my room was, I noticed a beautiful, bikini-clad young woman sitting on the outside steps—sunbathing, I presumed. She was very attractive, and I had not seen her in the previous weeks.

I retrieved what I was after and turned to leave the room. Glancing at the bikini-clad woman, I noticed her smiling at me. We greeted each other and I was off to work. To say I didn't spend some thought on that chance meeting would be a lie. However, I was a married man and was able to put the image of this young lady to the back of my mind.

Somewhat.

In a camp with nearly eighty men, word travelled fast about this new woman working for Majestic as a cleaner and cook's helper. We already had one young lady working in that capacity, Sandy, but it was too much work for just one person. As the days went on, I heard about all of the guys who were shot down and denied their opportunity to hook up with the new girl, prompting rumours of her being a lesbian.

About a week after my first encounter with her, I started to find that my bed was being made with a full sheet change every day. This was not common. Sheet changes only happened once a week. Opening my closet one evening after work, I noticed that all my laundry had been washed and folded, and was sitting neatly on the bottom shelf.

Somewhat confused, I mentioned this to my roommate— back then we shared a room in camps. He was surprised and commented, "I guess Sandy is increasing her assault on you to get you to sleep with her." True, Sandy had shown a great deal of desire to bed me. In fact, when my roommate and I would jam with my guitar and his banjo, Sandy would come, ostensibly to listen, and then lie on my bed in very provocative ways. I would have to physically remove her by as late as midnight so I could go to sleep. Don't get me wrong, Sandy was a good lookin' girl, but I was married. As much as I love beautiful women, I was *married!*

The next morning after breakfast, I confronted Sandy and explained that although I appreciated the nice gestures, I would appreciate it even more if she would cease and desist doing me any special favours because nothing was going to come of it. She laughed and informed me that it was not her but the new girl who was doing the special things for me. "Maybe you should talk to her," she added.

All that day I mused on what Sandy told me. I was flattered and bewildered. Why would this gorgeous woman be interested in me? I was nothing special. I was married with children as well—although she probably didn't know that. We had not had one word of conversation other than a hello on the first day we met. Not sure how to approach her and not even knowing her name, I procrastinated on dealing with the situation. I was afraid of what might happen if I pursued getting to know her. I think I was worried that she would shut me down and the rejection would be devastating.

One warm summer evening my roommate and I and a few buddies decided we would have a bit of a jam session and have a few soda pops made from barley. We were jamming and having a good time when I saw the beautiful woman walk past our room, look in briefly, then carry on. After an hour or so, and during a rousing rendition of "Cripple Creek," I broke a G-string on my guitar.

I had no replacements left but remembered that one of my other guitar-playing buddies told me if I ever needed strings, the drawer in his room was full of spares. Eric was away on holidays, but we never locked our rooms as we could trust our workmates back then. Eric's room was near the centre of our complex. I ran down the hall, turned the door handle and walked right in.

There, lying on the bed, or at least sitting up on the bed with the blankets pulled down to her waist, was this gorgeous young woman. I was a little startled, and could not help but stare at her beautifully proportioned breasts, concealed only by a sheer top that left nothing to the imagination!

I looked away, apologizing for coming into her room. "I thought it was Eric's," I said.

To which she calmly replied, "That's okay. Eric used to have this room but he quit two days ago and I was assigned his room." She added, "Can I help you with anything?"

"I was just going to grab a spare guitar string he said he had in the night table drawer."

"The strings are still in the drawer, so help yourself," she said.

I did and quickly left. I walked slowly back to my room, unable to get the image from my mind—her beautiful, inviting smile, her exceptional breasts. Remember, I was a young, hot-blooded man of not yet twenty-two. Although the blood in my cardiovascular system seemed to be working in only one part of my anatomy, I knew I was a married man and had made a promise to be faithful, no matter how sweet or exhilarating the moment may have been.

One week later, I was flying out of Dawson back to Vancouver Island for my days off. We would have one more thirty-day shift left and Majestic's Dempster Highway contract would be finished. Lynne and the kids, plus my youngest brother Lory, would join me heading back. We would drive with the truck and camper to the Yukon, and when my job was done we would holiday on our way back down the Alaska Highway.

Time flew by after we returned to the Yukon. My family spent the month exploring Dawson City and the surrounding area, rich with historical relics of the Gold Rush, and marvelling at the endless daylight. My job wound down and soon it was time to go. The last day in camp, with the family loaded into the truck, I went back to the shop for a final goodbye. After handshakes and hugs I headed back to the truck. As I passed the complex I'd stayed in, I decided to check my old room one last time to make sure I had everything.

I entered at the north side and was striding down the hallway when I came into the concourse junction. The beautiful young woman, who was like a mystery, met me as she was coming from the west end of the complex. Seeing me in my good clothes, she excitedly yet with some concern asked me what I was doing. I told her my work with Majestic was finished. Even though there was still about a week or two of breakdown and site cleanup to do, I was heading home.

She pleaded with me not to go, encouraging me to stay until the job was complete. I told her I was sorry, but it was time for me to go. Tears were streaming down her cheeks as I reached out to shake her hand goodbye, but instead she stepped forward and threw her arms around me. I could feel her trembling against me, pulling me closer to her. She kissed me on my lips.

I had never felt such love and passion in a simple kiss. I was overwhelmed. I wanted to stay in her arms and not let the moment end. Coming back to my senses, I realized I was kissing a beautiful stranger with my wife only a short distance away. I pushed her away from me, took one last look into her tear-filled eyes and left. I knew by then what a kiss driven by lust and desire felt like, but that day in 1977, I discovered what a kiss of true passion and love felt like. It was indescribable!

(Love may be the most misused word in any language. But when all your life you have wanted nothing more than to feel truly loved, the first time you feel the way I did that day, time is nothing but an abstract concept, and how long you've known each other has little significance compared with the magnitude of your feelings. At that moment, I felt no lust, as gorgeous as she was; maybe it was not love, but it felt like love to me.)

I have tried over the years to find out who she was, to no avail. I would love to be able to hug her again and tell her what that moment meant to me. I hope she is having a wonderful life. Thank you so much, beautiful lady. I will never forget you!

Ahhh... Fresh Air and Scary Bear

In the 1970s bow-hunting was exceptional, the deer populations were strong and chances of a kill were good, but that would only last for another few years before a drastic change took place. Until that happened, however, opening day of bow-hunting season usually saw me and my two buddies, Bob and Darrell, out on the first morning hunt.

At season's opening one year, we had already agreed on a place out north of Kelsey Bay on Vancouver Island, where we had done some early-season scouting. We had seen some decent shootable bucks a few days back.

The opening was on a Saturday, so Friday after work we loaded up the truck. We stopped on our way out to Adam River just long enough for Darrell to pick up a case of off-sales and grab a few pickled eggs at the Haida Inn bar.

It was about a one-and-a-half-hour drive to where we were going to set up camp for the weekend. Not long after we'd left, the pickled eggs and whatever else Darrell had eaten began to protest. An odorous flatulence required us to drive with the windows down for the last forty minutes or so. When we arrived, Bob and I bolted from the truck, finally able to get some much-needed unpolluted oxygen.

We set up the eight-by-eight-foot canvas tent, had a quick meal of mac and cheese with pork and beans, then headed out. Again we saw a few bucks in the area we had scouted earlier, so we were confident that tomorrow would bring a good morning.

We lit a small campfire and had a couple of beers. Unfortunately, the effects of Darrell's pickled eggs, now accompanied by beer and beans, did not subside but increased in frequency and volatility. Bob and I jockeyed around the campfire, trying desperately to stay upwind of Darrell.

It was getting late, almost midnight, and if we were planning to be successful with our pointed sticks in the morning, we needed to get to sleep—4:30 a.m. would come early.

We laid out our bags and crawled in. We all laid with our feet facing the tent opening. However not long into the night, Darrell was still expending copious amounts of toxin into the atmosphere. Being positioned in the middle, I swapped ends so my head was now at the tent opening. With the tent flap half open, I could get some relief from the rank smell. Bob and Darrell had already been fast asleep for about an hour.

I was on the verge of sleep myself when a noise outside the tent jolted me back to full consciousness. I lay motionless, listening hard, but my breathing seemed so loud I imagined it could be heard a hundred metres away. I could hear something shuffling about outside to my left. I looked over to see a large silhouette moving alongside the tent in the moonlight, toward the front of it. I knew it was a black bear paying us a visit. I wasn't sure if it was there because of the remaining smell of our evening supper or the smell of rotting flesh that Darrell was letting forth. Either way, I could not see the silhouette anymore.

Maybe he'd left, I hoped. Suddenly the question of where the bear had gone was answered. I felt a cold nose touch the back of my head through the open tent flap. I heard short breaths and felt each exhalation on my head. Petrified, I would not have moved even if I could have. This investigation of me was to last only a few moments, but it was the longest few moments of my life at that time. The bear, satisfied or disinterested, was gone as abruptly as he had appeared.

Sleep eluded me that night. When dawn was starting to break, I woke Bob and Darrell and told them of the late-night visitor. They laughed and said, "Sure you did." I insisted it had happened but they continued to doubt me—until we opened the flap of the tent to see fresh bear tracks right at the opening. Thankfully, by the end of the day the effects of Darrell's diet had subsided, and that night I was able to sleep with my head at the other end of the tent.

Swim! Swim!

The scorching July sun beat down on us relentlessly. Even the shaded areas I found around the house could not provide any relief from the unseasonably hot onslaught. Drinking water and wet towels, which dried out in mere minutes, could not assuage the desert-like conditions. Campbell River may not be Arizona in July, but it can get toasty warm when it has a mind to.

Finally, unable to stand it any longer, I decided a raft trip down the Campbell River was the needed remedy. I loaded my little two-man rubber/vinyl raft into the truck. I decided to bring my wolf-dog Muncho along, seeing that the heat was just as stifling for him as for me. He looked like he was about to expire, with his tongue hanging limply out of his mouth and panting like a steam locomotive pulling grade. Just as I was beginning to drive out of the yard, I noticed the young neighbour boy, Tom. He was about twelve years old and a nice lad. Sometimes I would go over to Tom's place and play flag football or soccer with him and all the other kids from the Oyster River neighbourhood.

As I noticed him he saw me, waved feebly and smiled. Tom, too, was feeling the heat and boredom of this sultry Saturday in July. Stopping the truck, I hollered to him to see if he wanted to go rafting with me.

Enthusiastically he yelled, "Yes! I'll ask my parents." He disappeared into the house, then moments later came running out, a big grin on his face. He jumped into the truck and thanked me profusely.

After arriving at the power station parking area, which is where we would launch from, we unloaded the inflatable raft. I gave it a few more good breaths of air before we headed to the river about ten metres below, with Muncho charging ahead. He would normally follow along the shoreline where he could or swim around any obstacles that he might encounter. Usually when we reached the point where the Quinsam River flowed into the Campbell River, we would pull out, walk back up to the truck, then do it again.

The water level was not that high, and they were not releasing a lot of water from the John Hart Dam. This would make some of the fast runs a little more treacherous if you fell out of the raft. The shallow water in places might only be half a metre deep. This, coupled with fast rapids, could make swimming almost impossible. You would be nearly completely at the mercy of the river as you rolled and bounced along the rock-strewn bottom.

We arrived at the bank with everything we needed: the raft and one small paddle for me to control our direction—somewhat. I would aim for some of the big rocks where the water would pile up, then we would drop over into the hydraulic pool on the other side and splash and bounce in the hole until we got shot out. I never wore life jackets, or for that matter even had them. After all, I was a strong swimmer and had done this countless times. Looking back now, how foolish that was. I didn't even know how well Tom could swim, or even whether he could.

Tom hopped in and I gave a little push, climbed in and away we went. As we slowly worked out of the little back eddy that we started from and entered the river's main channel, our speed began to increase exponentially. All was going as planned, the cool water splashing us with its refreshing and heat-absorbing qualities. Muncho, content to follow along the bank as usual, kept a close eye on our progress. Then, without warning, he dove headlong into the river and began a deliberate approach toward us.

Fearing the outcome of a sixty-eight-kilo wolf-dog wanting to enter our flimsy little raft with claws that could shred it like tissue paper, I yelled above the noise of the river, "Go back!" but he kept swimming in our direction. He was within a couple metres of the raft as we entered the shallow rapids. I knew it would be a dangerous, if not fatal, situation if we lost the buoyancy of the raft. I tried to push Muncho away with my paddle, but like a slick-footed boxer he dodged my thrusts and caught hold of the raft. With his one failed attempt to crawl into the raft, it ruptured.

Instantly we were banging and rolling in the deadly rapids. I crawled and swam as best I could toward the closest bank, which was only about fifteen metres or so away. Swallowing great gulps of water while trying to breathe, I choked and sputtered until I found the shore, with Muncho alongside. Suddenly I realized I could not see young Tom.

I looked downriver and caught sight of his almost lifeless body bobbing in the water. It rose for a brief moment, then rolled back under. His arms, with almost no strength remaining, feebly reached toward the shore. Screaming encouragement and fearing for his life, I could only say one thing: "Swim!

Swim!" I was helpless to do anything but scream those words, over and over.

With what seemed like a resurgence of strength and a renewed resolve, Tom began a half-swimming, half-crawling manoeuvre toward the shore. Running over the round beach rocks and slipping and falling as I went, I arrived at the same time that Tom made it to safety. I grabbed him by his limp forearms and dragged him farther onto the dry land. We both lay still for five minutes, gasping for air and waiting for the strength to return to our battered bodies.

With our strength back but our nerves still badly shaken, we headed back up along the Gold River Highway to our launching place by the power station. We didn't say a word to each other until we arrived back at the truck. Turning to Tom, I pleaded for his forgiveness for nearly taking his life because of my very foolish lack of safe preparation. He accepted my apology without qualification.

We headed home and never spoke of the incident again, neither I nor Tom. In fact, without any encouragement from me, Tom never did tell his parents—at least, not as long as we were neighbours!

That Sinking Feeling

Campbell River in the '70s was the premier salmon fishing destination in the world. Throw in summers that were usually balmy and warm and it was truly a glorious place to call home. Tourists especially loved it as they were only there for the summer. They missed out on the late fall weather, which began with southeasters and was followed with *rain, rain, rain!* The locals took solace in the fact that this would only last until mid-June of the next year.

During those summers, I was employed as a fishing guide for Lossette's Boat Rentals, which was located at the government wharf. We were extremely busy, some days arriving at the dock at 4:00 a.m. to prepare to take out the first party of the day by 4:30 a.m. Our guiding parties were usually scheduled for three hours but four-hour trips were more the norm as summer progressed. I think the charter companies wanted to make more money, but also give the guides a little more time to possibly catch some fish—after all, coming back with no fish is not good for business.

We would usually get a short break in the afternoon for a couple of hours to snooze. Sometimes it meant throwing a few life jackets across the seats of the fourteen-foot fibreglass boats we used and sleeping in the afternoon heat. Most days I would arrive home late in the evening after the last fishing party was finished. Wrapping up included weighing and cleaning·the clients' fish and prepping the boats for the next day. I would sometimes arrive home after midnight, get three hours' sleep and do it all again in the morning.

Ray was one of the guides I worked with, and he was given the moniker "Tyee Ray." He earned this name because of his ability to catch tyee, which are large chinook salmon, but more precisely because of his constant drone about always being able to get a tyee.

After one very hot and productive tide over at Whiskey Point, located near the entrance to Quathiaski Cove on Quadra Island, I was returning from the morning's charter. Arriving back at the dock around 10:00 a.m., I cleaned my clients' fish, bid them a good day and decided to take a quick nap before my next fishing party arrived. As if we had not had enough fishing already, Ray came over to my boat, where I was about to slumber in the warm July sun, and suggested that he and I go back out and fish the flood at Whiskey Point. Being an eager fisherman, I gave up my nap—albeit reluctantly—and agreed. Although if I had known what was going to transpire in a short while, I most definitely would have declined his invitation.

We jumped into Ray's boat and headed out. When we got to Whiskey Point, ten or more boats were already working the tide rip that was building. Some of those rips could get pretty angry, and you had to be in control all the time, with other boats to avoid and whirlpools opening up without any warning. It must have been quite an active spectacle as we jockeyed our way through each drift.

Usually there were no serious ˙incidents, although I do remember a couple of times where a guide and his party ended up capsized and a quick rescue ensued. On another occasion a middle-aged man had a heart attack from sheer terror when a large whirlpool opened up. They rushed him back to the government dock, with paramedics waiting. Unfortunately they were unable to revive the gentleman.

Ray and I were going to use live herring, or livies, as we called them. We had a short length of rope attached to the back of the boat with a bait pail on the other end. This would keep our live herring fresh and robust.

We manoeuvred into position among the other boats. The guides and experienced fishermen followed a protocol as to where you positioned yourself for the start of your drift to the fishing hole. We would begin our drift at the top of the tide rip, then slowly go with the current through the hole. We put out our lines and got ready for action, and we definitely were going to get it.

As we drifted through the tide rip, nearing the tail end of it, a huge whirlpool suddenly developed. At first we were not too concerned. We had experienced them many times. The pool continued to grow, but we were still confident that as fast as it had appeared it would dissipate.

It did not. It continued to get bigger and more intense. We hurriedly reeled in our lines, and Ray put the 20 HP Evinrude into gear. It lurched forward then stopped.

Looking back to see what had happened, Ray pulled at the short rope tied to our bait bucket, only to find it was wound tight around our propeller.

We no longer had any power and were now at the mercy of the ever-expanding whirlpool. We began to orbit around, building speed as it dragged us closer to the eye of the vortex like some great monster of the deep, savouring the first taste of the meal it was soon to devour.

The centre of the pool began to drop. I was sitting in the bow of the boat, thinking that the farther I was from the vortex, the less likely it would be that I would be sucked down to my death.

At this point we could no longer see any of the boats that had surrounded us just moments earlier. Looking into the clear smooth waters of the whirlpool, I could see logs, driftwood and debris as far as seven or eight metres down. Ray rushed to the bow of the boat, shoving his back against my chest and screaming, "We're going to die!" over and over. "We're going to die!" was all he could say. What little hope I had prior to him screaming of our impending grisly death was now completely gone. This was it. We were going to die!

Then, above the swirling hiss and breath of that watery demon, a voice yelled, "They're in a hole!" Moments later the same voice ordered, "Grab the rope!" An instant later I felt a rope fall across my head. I reached up and grabbed the rope, still in a state of shock, holding it in my shaking hands until I again heard the voice scream above the noise of the rip tide, "Tie it off!" Coming to my senses, I pushed hard to get Ray away from me, then turned to the bow to tie it off on what I thought would be a bow cleat.

There was no cleat! There was only a small aluminum plate riveted to the bow, approximately fifteen centimetres deep and forty wide. I wrapped the rope around both my wrists, then jammed them under the aluminum plate. At nearly the same moment, the rope tightened and I heard the sound of twin 90 HP Mercruisers powering up.

In an instant the slack was gone from the rope. The boat was equipped with flotation; however, we had taken in a great deal of water and the stern was now submerged in the ocean. We soon would have capsized and been drawn down to our demise in Davy Jones's Locker.

As the other boat was trying to pull us to freedom, it too became caught in the arc of the whirlpool's deadly grip. I felt another great pull on my already taxed arms as another boat hooked onto the struggling boat that had first came to our aid. Gradually we made some headway—round and round we went until I could see our rescuers. It was as though the monster had decided we were no longer worth the fight, disappeared into the dark depths and was gone.

The heroes towed us to shore with now only about ten centimetres of freeboard left. We beached the boat and began to bail out the hundreds of litres of water. With that task finally completed and the rope untangled from the motor, Ray, with obviously no memory of what had just transpired, asked with enthusiasm, "You want to finish fishing the tide?" In utter disbelief, I answered, "Are you out of your bloody mind? Head this damn boat back to the dock—I'm done fishing!"

That was the first and last time I ever spent free time fishing with Tyee Ray!

The Flying Apple Crate

When I was a young boy of seven or eight years of age, I wasn't much good at anything. When I played road hockey with my brothers—if they let me play—I was always the goalie. As goalie, back then, you were just someone to shoot the puck at. The puck consisted of a round orange-sized rock, stuffed into a work sock, rolled into a ball, then taped with electrician's tape. I think I must have been good at it because I took a lot of pucks in the face, and everywhere else. If we played baseball, I was always right field because hardly anyone hit a ball to right field.

But none of that mattered when I dreamed about the one thing I wanted more than anything else. I wanted to be able to fly, to soar over the trees and fields, to simply be free. I wanted to go gliding through the skies, with no motor. I would fly low over all the kids in my neighbourhood when they were playing baseball or road hockey. They would see how great I was, flying in my amazing flying machine that I designed and built all by myself. It would operate using all the magic that a child's vivid imagination could conceive.

At that age, I mumbled more than talked and stuttered quite a bit. They said I mumbled and stuttered so much that nobody could understand a word I said, but that was okay because one day they would see how famous I would become.

I would be known all around the world as the greatest adventurer and inventor ever.

Early one Saturday morning on a sunny and beautiful day, I decided it was time to build my very own airplane. I had dreamed about exactly how it would be built. I quietly borrowed some of my dad's tools. I should have asked first, but I knew he would think I couldn't do it, especially all by myself. I also had the most important item: an apple box from Aunt Marie. She was going to burn it for a summer wiener roast until I pleaded with her to let me have it. Aunt Marie was always nice to me.

I had some nails and a couple of pieces of scrap plywood left over from building the garage on our little house. I found some string that had been used to hold hay bales together. I now had everything I needed except some wheels for my plane. I would figure that out when the time came.

Before anyone was out of bed, I gathered all my materials together and put them in my wagon. Out I headed into the forested hillside above and across from our home. It was to be a secret, so nobody would steal my invention. What a surprise it would be when I soared through the skies above everyone below!

I cut plywood and nailed boards, and before long it looked something like the plane I had dreamed about. Now if only I had some wheels, it would be complete. I lay on a grassy hill to contemplate where I could get my much-needed wheels. Looking down on our neighbourhood, I saw that people were now up and about at their weekend outdoor activities.

Mr. Gruzzly was cutting his lawn. The fat lady across the road was hanging out her laundry. I never knew her name;

everyone just called her the fat lady. Kids started coming out and gathering near the street. I munched on an apple and some peanut butter cookies Mom had made (Mom always made really good cookies). As I lay there, I watched everyone out enjoying the warm summer morning.

Still wondering where I could find some wheels to put on my plane, it suddenly came to me: my wagon. *Yes!* The wagon had wheels. I could use them. There was only one important detail that would be a problem. The wagon was a Christmas gift that I had to share with one of my older brothers, Terry.

I knew what I would do. When I finished flying my super-special plane, I would just put the wheels back on the wagon. Terry would never even know. That way he wouldn't beat me up—unless he found out, and I knew he wouldn't.

Once the wheels were attached and I checked that everything was tight and in place, it was time to take my first flight. Feeling a bit nervous and not totally confident now that it was time to really fly, I convinced myself that my faith was greater than any challenge. It would overcome all obstacles. To defy and control gravity would be my reward and victory.

I had already picked the perfect place to start my downhill descent, a steep portion of the hill that ended at a natural abrupt lip jutting out and up over the grassy hillside below. I watched people coming out to enjoy the sunshine, some doing chores, others playing. As was the tradition, all the neighbourhood kids were gathering on the Wilsons' vacant lot for a game of baseball. Soon the lot was full of kids playing ball. They were completely unaware of the monumental feat they would soon witness.

Getting into position, I blocked the back wheels with a rock to hold my flying machine in place until I gained enough courage. I took one last long breath of air, climbed in, reached down to the rock that held me captive to the earth and pulled it away. I began my descent. Faster and faster I sped. I said a silent prayer, hit the lip of the hill that would launch me into the skies above—and *swoosh!* I was flying!

I soared up and over the field below. Still no one had seen me and my marvellous flying apple crate, but now they would. I banked hard on the broken broomstick handle that was my control, gliding silently toward the Wilsons' lot. Flying low over the field, I heard gasps of wonder, shouts of "What is that? Who is that?" I leaned out over the side of my apple crate and waved to the kids below.

They could not believe their eyes. It was Kelly the mumbler, the kid who never got picked to be on the team. Yes, it was *me* flying through the air. I heard cheering and praise for what I had accomplished. I even buzzed Mr. Gruzzly as he was cutting his lawn, flying low over his head. He shook his fist at me, but I could see a smile forming on his face.

Uncle Edward was gardening in his backyard. I flew close to say good morning. He waved excitedly and asked, "Are you the man that pushed the bull over the bridge?" I never knew why he said that, he just always did. Finally, it was time to land, and I glided down on the big grassy field that bordered our neighbourhood and the Wilsons' lot.

Everyone came running to me and patted me on the back. The older people shook my hand. They were all smiling and happy. Everyone wanted to be my best friend and for me to be first pick for their teams. The newspaper crew arrived, and they took pictures of me and my wonderful apple crate airplane. Everyone loved me and didn't care that I was weird, too young or mumbled and talked funny. Even my brother Terry said he was proud of me, and he wasn't a bit mad at me for taking the wheels off our wagon.

That dream was a long time ago. Sometimes I wish I could go back to being a child again.

Buried at Sea

The first trip with my father that I can recall happened when I was six years old. My dad worked at Theodosia Inlet, situated in Desolation Sound on the south coast of British Columbia. He was Cat-logging a steep, hilly section near the head of the inlet.

On Monday morning at the Tyee seaplane dock we launched the sixteen-foot aluminum boat, loaded with some groceries, fuel and other items needed for our stay at camp. I was going to be spending a week with Dad until school started in September.

The trip over was kind of fun until we got near the southeast tip of Quadra Island, where it began to get quite choppy. But we continued across the open channel, rounding the south end of Cortes Island with still a good ways to go. I became soaked from the wind-whipped spray raining down as we ploughed into each wave. After what seemed like an eternity, we finally arrived at the camp.

We hauled the groceries and all the other gear to the camp and dried ourselves out. Dad made us supper and we both devoured it because we had not eaten anything since 5:00 a.m. For a six-year-old, that seemed like an eternity. I know now that the trip must have taken at least four hours as we battled the wind and tide.

That evening after supper Dad took me up the hill—a steep and rocky grade—on the D6 dozer to where he was logging and building road. Dad would skid the big timber down to the beach. On high tide, once the logs floated free of the mud, he would tow them into booms.

After that, we got in the boat and went out on the tidal flat, which was now covered with three metres or more of water as the tide came in. It was dark, so Dad brought a big flashlight that he shone into the water below. I could see it was alive with all kinds of strange and wonderful things swimming, crawling or, in the case of the jellyfish, floating along as if defying the aquatic gravity. It was both eerie and fascinating.

The next morning came quickly—I could hardly remember even going to bed. Dad told me we were going to visit some folks who lived up at a little farm about one and a half kilometres farther up the inlet.

We ate breakfast and cleaned up our dishes before grabbing a few items Dad wanted to drop off. He fired up the D6 dozer. While it was warming up, he led me over to another dozer sitting near the makeshift shop. It was an old Allis-Chalmers, a little smaller than the D6 and I think even older.

Pointing to the weather-beaten seat, he said, "Hop aboard." I climbed up onto the seat, not sure exactly why, until he started to give me instructions on how to operate it. He showed me how to engage the drive system for forward and reverse, how to turn it, then how to stop. That was it. Then he fired it up. It barked and sputtered for a moment, then roared to life.

Dad jumped off and climbed aboard his dozer. Above the roar of the motor, he hollered for me to follow him across the mud flats. The tide had almost fully ebbed, and we had around three hours before it would hinder us from coming back to camp later in the morning. Then just like that he was gone. He jumped into the D6 and started across the flats. I sat there frozen in fear, both fear of this noisy belching iron beast and fear of being left behind.

He looked back only once, motioned for me to get following him, and then never looked back again. That was how Dad taught whatever we needed to learn. You had to pay attention because you were not going to get too many chances to figure things out. I now knew why he had me go up the hill on the D6 with him the night before, and I knew enough to watch every move he made. He was preparing me for today.

As he became more distant, fear was overcome by need— the need to follow as instructed or disappoint him. By this time Dad was about two hundred metres ahead of me. I engaged the master clutch and jerked forward as I headed down to the mud flats. I jerked on the left steering clutch, which locked the track on the left side, and with the right track still driving, turned the machine to trace the same course Dad had just set. Now I simply had to follow his tracks.

When I was halfway across, I began to think about the previous night, watching the ocean life floating across the very area that I was now traversing with a dozer. Suddenly, frightful thoughts entered my mind. *What if the old machine quits running? Or the tide comes in at a moment's notice?* I would be doomed to drown and all those creatures that filled the ocean in the dark of night would come and devour my body as a punishment for not leaving with Dad and keeping up with him.

I pulled back on the throttle once again to make sure I was going as fast as I could. Dad was still two hundred metres or so ahead and had still not looked back. Did he not care that I might be swallowed by the sea and die as an unwilling sacrifice?

Finally, at the end of the inlet, Dad and his D6 came out of the flats and up onto hard ground and he looked back in my direction at last. I couldn't tell from that distance but I think he was smiling just a bit. We arrived at the farm, visited with the lady who was there and enjoyed a big piece of fresh apple pie. We then said our goodbyes and headed back to our own place.

Driving the dozer across the mud flats this time, I stayed right behind my dad. As we crossed I could see the tide was coming in and the flats were receding. The tide continued to overtake the bay, but I was no longer afraid. I was victorious and now confident that I would be recognized as a full-fledged and fully experienced cat skinner!

Over the years I have worked with dozers in all kinds of precarious situations. Some places were so steep that I was nearly defying the law of gravity. It often gave onlookers and employees of mine near heart attacks. I guess I have to thank (or blame) my dad for that. If he'd had all that confidence in me at six years of age, what is there that I couldn't do with a dozer now?

Golf Balls and Rattlesnakes

My mother did her best to feed and clothe us growing up, all eight of us; however, giving us allowance or spending money was simply not in the family budget. I collected bottles, and back in the '60s there wasn't much else a kid could do for money. When you had a sack full of bottles worth fifty cents, you were toting thirteen kilograms of bottles, not like now when most are lightweight aluminum cans. It was hard work to earn enough for a special treat, like a big homestyle hamburger with all the fixings, washed down with a nice big frosty milkshake—still a great deal at $1.75 for both. But it took a lot of two-cent bottles to reach that!

It was 1968, school had just ended and my buddy Richard and I were anxious to start earning some much-needed spending money, but collecting bottles was too much work and definitely not a big enough payday for the effort. Being only twelve years old, we were struggling to find work. The cherries were in harvest but the orchards in our area wouldn't hire us kids until we were high school age. As that was the most popular and readily available employment, most of the kids from high schools in Rutland, where we lived, or Kelowna, right down Highway 97, pretty much had all the picking jobs sewn up.

We had made a little money using our pellet guns to shoot starlings for the orchardists. We got twenty-five cents per set of legs. This helped out from May to midsummer, but the birds seemed to become cagier as spring turned to summer. Our success rate dropped off considerably then, so back on went our thinking caps. Surely there was some way we hadn't thought of yet that would help us earn some real money.

One afternoon, as I hiked into Kelowna to go to the park for a swim in Okanagan Lake, I passed by the Mountain Shadows Golf Course. The first couple of fairways were right beside Highway 97 (which later became known as Harvey Avenue) through town. As I was walking past, a golf ball bounced in front of me and as it was heading for the highway I reached out quick as a cat and grabbed it. Thinking that was pretty neat, I stuffed it into my pants pocket.

Almost immediately, someone yelled out from the fairway as he ran toward me, "Hey kid, that's my ball. You want to give it back?" More of a demand than a question. Not knowing what I would do with it, I grabbed the ball out of my pocket, tossed it gently onto the fairway and continued on. The golfer then shouted, "Hey, wait a minute."

I thought, *What does he want? I gave his ball back. Maybe I should start running.* Just as I was about to flee, the man hollered, "Here, take this," as he reached his hand out with a quarter for me. "Thanks, kid. Buy yourself something." I gratefully accepted his offering and carried on to the lake.

Heading home a few hours later, as I was passing the golf course it suddenly dawned on me how Richard and I could make some good money. I knew that people always hit golf balls off the course because I'd seem them lying on the road and in ditches, and I figured if we went on the back side of the course, where it bordered Knox Mountain, we could probably find lots of balls there. Plus that area was all fenced with barbed wire and, considering how many balls I had seen lying in the grass and along the ditch bordering Highway 97, it was obvious the golfers did not like to make any effort to retrieve their balls or even leave the course.

The next morning Richard and I were down at the course looking in the tall grass along the adjoining railroad tracks. There were three fairways along that northwest side—we would do well along there, I thought. When we arrived around 10:00 a.m., plenty of golfers were out. All we needed now was to find lots of golf balls.

And we did find lots of balls. Within twenty minutes we found at least twenty golf balls. Some were a little chewed up. (Later, as we became more knowledgeable, we would appropriately call them "smileys" because of the smile-shaped cut carved by a misplaced hit.) Richard and I quickly did the math, twenty balls at twenty-five cents each—after all, that was what the guy had given me the day before—would add up to $5. That was more than two hard days of bottle collecting could earn, and we didn't have to lug a fifteen- to twenty-kilogram sack of bottles all over the place.

I wasn't sure what to say to the golfers who would occasionally glance over at these two young boys standing in the tall grass on the other side of the fence; some had concerned looks on their faces. Nevertheless, I gathered enough courage to walk up to the fence as three golfers were walking up the fairway, still looking at us in a sort of disbelief. I hollered, "Do you want to buy some golf balls? Only twenty-five cents each."

The three men unanimously said yes. "Sure, what have you got?" asked one of them. I thought that was strange, so I just told them, "Golf balls!" To which the same fellow said, "I know that, but what kind, what make?"

I looked at the three balls I was holding and noticed they had names on them, such as Titleist and Wilson. Now I understood. As I was about to say the names, the closest guy said, "Let me have a look," and I held out my hand to him.

He looked at the three in my hand, nodded and said, "I'll take this one," pointing to the Titleist. I handed him the ball and he handed me a quarter.

The other two asked, "Do you have any more?"

I quickly answered, "Yes." We opened a plastic bag with the rest of the balls. The men looked inside and picked up a couple to look over.

One fellow exclaimed, "Hey, there are a few one-hitters in here." Looking at Richard and me, he offered to take three for fifty cents.

"Sure!" I replied. The fellow took two more for thirty-five cents.

We had four smileys in the bunch. The golfer who bought the Titleist offered me another quarter for those four smileys. He said he used them when he was hitting over sneaky water traps because he didn't mind losing a smiley in the water. Then they said goodbye and away they went. Richard and I were grinning from ear to ear. We'd made $1.35 in twenty minutes and we had only started.

More golfers came by throughout the day; some told us to get lost but most either said not now or came and purchased balls from us. We managed to sell all our golf balls. Then we found another bunch of balls, not sure how many the second time, and they too all sold. We had earned nearly seven bucks in less than two hours. Considering minimum wage was $2.25 per hour for the average working person, we thought we had hit the motherlode!

Ready to reward ourselves with deluxe burgers and milk-shakes, we headed over to the little burger joint across the highway from the golf course. As we enjoyed our morning success and burgers, I remembered something one of the first group of golfers had said—that he used the smileys when he was hitting over sneaky water traps. I told Richard, "I bet there are thousands of balls in the water traps along the north-west side of the course." We agreed that the next morning we would be there before the sun was up and sneak onto the course, wade into those water holes and see how many balls we could find.

Early in the pre-dawn light we were already on the course and pulling ball after ball out of the muddy bottoms of the water traps. We were nearly finished what we thought was a thorough search on the first water trap on the fifth fairway when we heard someone yelling obscenities at us as he approached in a little green cart of some sort with a box on the back. He continued to threaten us, cursing a blue streak. We grabbed our running shoes, socks and our two bulging bags of golf balls and made for the safety of the fence and the railroad tracks. We climbed over the fence and ran to the tracks, about ten metres away. The irate man drove up to the fence and told us to keep our #$@&*$% asses off the course and don't come back!

We nodded in agreement and pretended to be leaving, after which, seemingly satisfied, he drove away. Once he was safely gone and out of our view, we set up at our spot along the fifth fairway by the fence. A half-hour later we had our first customers, and throughout the morning we carried on a brisk business, selling nearly all the balls we had found except for a few that were too damaged—we couldn't even sell them for a nickel. We had earned $14-plus that day in one hour of gathering balls and just over two hours of selling. Another fantastic day, but a record day was yet to come.

As the summer rolled on, some really nice golfers helped us figure out which balls were worth more than others. We began to know what the real values were for the different brands. Another golfer suggested that we go and clean the balls at the ball washer that was at the fifth fairway tee box, as that would help their value. He said, "It's all in the presentation."

One hot early August day found us once again searching for balls along the track, which was rimmed by knee-high dead summer grasses. We now had to cover a lot more range to find the quantity we needed, and make sure we were out of the water traps before the fellow in the green cart could see us. We later learned that he was the groundskeeper for Mountain Shadows.

We also finally found out why so many folks would stare at us across the fence near the tracks. One afternoon we were dickering with a potential buyer. We no longer simply sold golf balls for a quarter; in fact, some of the one-hits would fetch me seventy-five cents, depending on what type of ball it was. Another golfer approached the fellow from behind, saying, "You better be giving these kids a good price for those balls, considering the danger they're in gathering them." The fellow said, "Yeah, I guess you kids deserve a little danger pay." Neither Richard nor I had any idea what they were talking about. We certainly weren't afraid of the pot-bellied guy in the green cart—once we crossed the fence, he wouldn't come any closer than three metres.

As we finished our transaction, one of the fellows offered us a warning: "Watch out for them rattlers. That hill and tracks are loaded with them."

"What! Rattlesnakes?" Richard and I stared at him, dumbfounded. Was he joking? We had never seen a rattlesnake, but then we had not really been looking. We were transfixed on looking for round white objects, not snakes. At that point we'd had a good day, our best day yet, at over $25. We still had thirty balls left but decided we had plenty of money for the moment.

Hiding our bags of golf balls, we headed for the burger joint to eat our favourite meal and play the pinball machine. We took a week off from golf-ball hunting and went fishing and swimming in Mission Creek, playing like two normal twelve-year-olds. But soon we were broke and needed to earn money again to facilitate the lifestyle we had become accustomed to. I asked some folks about the so-called rattlesnake situation at Knox Mountain and along the train tracks, to which every answer was the same: "There are tons of rattlers along there!" What were we to do? If we collected bottles every day all year we wouldn't earn as much as we did collecting and selling golf balls in one good summer day.

Greed overcame fear, and in the wee hours we were back at the familiar water traps, collecting golf balls. It was as if during the week or so we were gone, every ball hit over those traps had fallen into the water. In less than one hour, with Richard in one trap and me in another, we had close to eighty balls, of which the majority were one-hits. We quickly and carefully jumped over the fence to be clear of the groundskeeper. Then we banged and raked the ground along the tracks with metre-long sticks, trying to find balls and also root out rattlesnakes. (We did find a rattle but no snakes.)

Much like in the water traps, we were finding huge numbers of balls on both sides of the tracks. When we finally decided we had more than enough, we began selling again from our normal retail spot along the fence. I'm not sure to this day how many balls we sold, but we sold all but a handful, from smileys to perfect one-hits. Business was booming and most of our customers were regulars, who by now knew that we knew the value of the balls, especially since I had recently paid a visit to the pro shop and got the prices that the shop sold them for.

On that day, we had a fairly big group of new golfers who were buying balls like they were the last ones left. A middle-aged man—at least he looked middle-aged to me, but he was probably thirty-five in reality—was trying to dicker me down to fifty cents on a quality Titleist ball that retailed for $1.25 in the pro shop. At that moment one of my regulars came over and suggested to the fellow, "Just pay him the seventy-five cents, the kid knows his golf balls." He not only bought the one but bought three more for the same price.

I had just made $2.25 for three balls. *Yes!*

At the hottest part of the day, around 2:30 p.m., it was slowing down a bit, but we kept making sales. By 4:00 p.m. it had become fairly quiet on the course, and we had only a handful of balls left. We decided it was time to count up our day's earnings; I was the salesman and treasurer. We hiked over into some shade trees on the north boundary of the course, with me constantly pulling my pants up from the weight of all the coins that bulged from all four pockets, and pulled out all the money, the coins along with wads of one- and two-dollar bills. Spreading it out on my T-shirt, I began to count, with Richard mimicking me counting. The coins first, then the bills. Finally, counting the last one-dollar bill, we could not believe what we saw. Simultaneously, we both let out a whoop and laughed.

On my T-shirt was the equivalent of finding a gold nugget the size of a golf ball! In total, $56 was laid out on my shirt. This was a king's ransom to a young and not-so wealthy boy, when a bottle of pop was twelve cents, a bag of chips was ten cents and you could eat like a king for $2.50. We split our earnings fifty-fifty and ate deluxe burgers, played pinball, ate some more deluxe burgers and washed them down with thick chocolate milkshakes right from the frosted metal container. Yes, life was good in the summer of '68.

We continued to collect golf balls for the rest of the summer. We never matched our performance on that fantastic, unbelievable day, but we never went hungry for a minute!

Once Bitten, Twice Shy

Crooked Lake, British Columbia: a pristine lake nestled at the base of the Cariboo Mountains, with Wells Gray Park's western boundary only a half-day ride by horseback. Sections near Eureka Peak, on the north side, hold little pockets of snow that can be a godsend in late summer—however, that's for another story.

My good friend Mary Morrison and her son Rob had recently purchased the hunting and guiding business known as Eureka Peak Guides & Outfitters, a few kilometres above Crooked Lake on the west side. The main cabin was not much for size or looks, kind of a ramshackle wood structure that housed a common room for meals and visiting, and a small bedroom that was home to more rodents than people. A few other rustic cabins dotted the clearing around the main camp. I think the outdoor toilet facilities were in better repair than the main building was.

Just in behind the camp was a small beaver lake where we got our water. Fortunately for us, we never experienced the abdominal and gastric problems associated with beaver fever. It was surprising considering the number of beavers that lived in the lodges on the small lake, evidenced by the copious amounts of beaver droppings on the bottom.

With her son still in school, Mary had asked me earlier in the week if I would be interested in helping get the camp back up and running. I agreed without hesitation. Mary was a great lady and treated me well. I didn't know quite how much work it was going to be until I got there.

Mary's boyfriend Roy was a lazy drunk, and I was about to find out just how lazy a drunk he was. Roy was going to be the ramrod, so to speak, so I would be taking my instructions from him. I was a single father back then, and my son Kelly would stay with Mary while I was gone for the week or so.

One Friday morning in early August, we were heading out to the camp. I would be riding out with Roy and our cook, Frenchie—who was also one of Roy's drinking buddies and just as lazy! We arrived not long after lunch and unloaded some of the gear and food from the truck. Roy took special care while unloading his case of whiskey.

After making myself some sandwiches, I took one of the little tin boats out on the beaver lake and tried some fishing. After a couple of hours of fruitless casting and trolling, I decided to call it quits.

The rest of the day I wandered around camp, doing a little exploring—mostly to kill time before going to bed, as I did not care much for Roy's company. I thought about asking him if I could use the truck to go to Crooked Lake, but I disliked him so much that I didn't even want to talk to him. Just after dark I laid out my bedroll on an old army cot, knowing we had a ton of work to do tomorrow.

I awoke just as the sun was making its appearance and already I could feel that it was going to be a scorcher. There wasn't even a wisp of a breeze, only blazing heat. We needed to get the corral fixed up and about an acre of land fenced that day. By noon the next day there would be between twelve and fourteen horses arriving to be unloaded and boarded, after which we would be training them for pack and saddle. Most of the horses were at least green broke, and some would have been ridden western; either way, they would have new roles to play here at Eureka Peak Guides & Outfitters.

I had a quick breakfast of bacon and eggs (Frenchie actually got up to cook), took one last long drink of water and suggested to Roy that we should get busy on that fencing. Roy enthusiastically answered, "You bet! The posts are all by the corral and so is the hand post pounder." I stood staring in disbelief and asked, "When are you planning to come help?" To which he said, while reaching down to massage an imaginary injury, "I can't do much. I have a bad back."

I could already feel the sweat starting to run down my back from the heat. Now I had anger to heat me up even more. I told myself, "This is for Mary and Rob, not for this lazy, pathetic drunk!"

Heading out to the corral, I found a large pile of two-metre fence posts. Lying beside the pile of posts was a special device designed to bring grown men to tears while breaking their backs, possibly the evillest thing ever created. It was a thirty-kilo handmade fence-post pounder, as long as your arm and twice the diameter, the pipe almost as thick as a man's thumb, with a skookum piece of two-centimetre flat plate welded to the end. When I finally talked myself into the task at hand, I started at the end of the ten-by-ten-metre corral nearest the gravel road that wound its way past the camp and down to Crooked Lake.

After sliding a post into the post pounder, I lifted and straightened the first post to pound it in. *Bang, bang, bang...*

over and over in that blazing sun I drove that pounder into the post. The ground was nothing but rock, packed and hardened by the season-long heat, which had welded those rocks together like concrete. After managing to put in three posts, I decided to count how many times I had to lift that thirty-kilo widow-maker, then drive it back down as forcibly as I could, to get them to the required depth of at least forty-five centimetres. I averaged sixty hits per post.

On and on I went. By 7:00 p.m., with only two short breaks to eat something and give my burning arms and shoulders a rest, I had forty-seven posts in and wired for the horses. I estimated I had hit those posts nearly 2,900 times, or lifted the equivalent of 85,802 kilos.

If that was all I'd had to do, I would have been satisfied and happy to head home. However, the next day had other plans for me. Waking early the next morning, I made my own breakfast of a couple cold-cut sandwiches. Frenchie and Roy were too hungover to even get up. They had put a serious beating on a couple of twenty-sixers of OFC's finest whiskey.

I got to repairing some of the bad rails on the corral, replaced some loose and busted boards on the loading ramp, and fixed the gate between the corral and the new fenced area I had built the previous day. I don't even know why we built that fence. The land was nothing but a rock pile with scarcely enough grass to feed one mangy rabbit.

I was putting the final touches on the corral when the open stock truck could be heard, then seen, rumbling into view. By this time Roy and Frenchie had arrived, and they instructed the driver to back up to the ramp and unload. As this was happening, I had a chance to see our guests for the next few months:

twelve horses that had seen better days, bug-eyed, wound tight like violin strings and not looking like they wanted to be here any more than I did. As the last bronc was unloaded they continued to kick, bite and generally show a great deal of animosity toward each other.

Roy handed me a box of halters, six different colours to identify the horses better. "They all need these halters on. If you use two of the same colour halters, just make sure the horses are different in colour to avoid confusion," he said, and off he and Frenchie went.

The dust had still not cleared, but the squeals were lessening now that the horses were in a slightly larger environment. Like opposing gangs settling in on their own sides of the turf, they were keeping a vigilant eye on each other. But at least they seemed to have settled enough for me to dare entering the corral.

I slowly manoeuvred up to each horse and gently but firmly placed on the appropriate halter. I felt things were going pretty good other than the odd knothead humpin' up in my direction, warning me to stay clear. I had managed to get nine halters on, but as it is with most things in life, just when you think you have everything under control, all hell breaks loose and you're scrambling to survive.

My overconfidence nearly cost me dearly as I strode toward a big bay gelding, feeling pretty good about myself. *Yes sir, Kelly, you sure do know your way around horses.* The gelding pinned his ears and made for me. I dove behind a couple of horses to my right, using them as a shield, then headed for the fence as I felt the brush of air and hoof across my pant leg.

I stood outside of the corral with three halters still to go. For reasons unknown to me, I climbed back in to finish the job. I spied that nasty devil of a gelding in behind a couple of mares, as calm as could be. I approached him while keeping a wary eye on two other mares off to my left. Slightly distracted, he seemed to think I was focusing on them—until I was able to reach out and short-mane him by the top of the head. I had him kind of boxed in and he quickly gave in to the halter.

I had two last mares to go, a big palomino and an appaloosa. The appy was close to where the loading ramp was. I grabbed a mare beside me that I had already haltered and used her as a block as I edged up to the appaloosa. It worked, and I was able to keep her wedged in by the ramp and my blocking horse.

Letting go of the mare, I grabbed the appy, and just as I was about to clasp the buckle I suddenly felt a searing pain go right through my shoulder and collarbone. That big bitch of a palomino bit down from behind me, grinding her teeth into my right shoulder, then picked me up off the ground like I was a rag doll. Then, loosening her grip on my jacket (luckily I had worn it for some protection from possible nips), she dropped me. Before she had a chance to get a better grip, I dove under the bottom rail of the corral, reached up to my now throbbing shoulder and felt the ooze of blood trickling down my T-shirt onto my chest and back.

I sat on a log under two young pine trees and contemplated my next move. It didn't take long to make up my mind. Heading back to the camp, I stamped in to see Roy and Frenchie, who were sucking the fumes out of another bottle of whiskey. In pain and mad as hell, I threw the remaining halter onto the table. It slid onto Roy's fat gut, and with all the emotion I felt at that moment, I told him, "There is one horse left. You can put the bloody thing on! I'm out of here!"

I stormed out, trying to figure out how I was going to get home. I had ridden up with Roy to the hunting camp. Right then a sheepish Frenchie came out and informed me that Roy was going to see Mary in 100 Mile House, so I could ride with them. I almost declined the offer for fear I might be charged with first degree murder or, at the very least, grievous assault.

A half-hour later, when they were ready to go, I had calmed down enough to make the three-hour trip. Not a word was said by Roy or Frenchie the whole way there. Good thing for them that they didn't!

Evergreen Warriors

Back in the day, when you wanted action and adventure, you didn't get it from TV, your computer or your phone. You made your own.

School had ended for another boring year, and summer holidays were about to start ramping up with all kinds of neat adventures: hiking, playing ball, fishing, go-kart racing down Evergreen Hill and squirrel hunting with pellet guns and .22s. It would be a relentless diet of adventure and fun. Sadly, this would be the year before our family, or at least me, my siblings and mother, would move to Kelowna. But before that happened, at seven years old I had an endless appetite for adventure, and I was about to get plenty.

This particular summer, most of us who lived around Evergreen Road and Dogwood in the southwest area of Campbell River, kind of the low-rent district, decided it would be cool to cut down a bunch of alder trees on a lot next to the Ordanos. They lived down from our place on the opposite side of Evergreen Road, and the adjoining lot had been empty for years. We never saw anyone ever go there, so we thought that there was nobody to mind. We all worked together, clearing a large area in the middle about twelve metres deep and nearly the full width of the lot, about eighteen metres or so wide.

The original plan, as well as I can remember, was that we would make forts on both the south and north sides, just for something to do. However, those plans started to change and evolve into something a little more sinister. Why not have two armies and have wars? My oldest brother Robin and his buddies would be on one side and my brother Sandy and all the younger kids would be on the other side. The younger kids would outnumber Robin's army, but they were older and bigger after all, so that would be fair, right?

We worked feverishly every day until we had the makings of a real battlefield. We younger kids constructed a short wall, nearly half a metre high and not quite a third of the way across the open area that we had cleared off, using the trees we cut down. This would act as a barrier to hide behind while we engaged Robin's team in battle.

Rules were simple: there really weren't any. We could use any weapon that we could make from the trees or branches or stones. Bow and arrow were the first choice, spears next and slingshots probably last. But we could not do any hand-to-hand combat, as Robin and his friends would have a distinct advantage over us.

After both teams had manufactured enough weapons of war and made our own unique flags to fly (not sure what they were now), we were ready for war. Early in the morning we would all gather at the lot, then go to our respective sides, like boxers going to their corners to wait for the bell to ring. The official start of the battle was also simple. Once the team flags were raised, the fight began.

The sky would be alive with all manner of projectiles flying overhead: spears, arrows and stones. You would hear them crashing and jamming themselves into the ground and rico-cheting off the remaining spindly trees that gave little cover from the onslaught. There would be shouts of pain as some of these missiles made their mark.

I was the youngest and could not throw the spears very far or shoot the homemade bows either. My job was to be the retriever. You may ask, what is a retriever? Simply put, my job was to hide behind our log barricade and wait for the barrage of arrows and spears to slow down in frequency. Then I would jump the barricade and, as fast as I could run, gather the spears and arrows that had not quite made it all the way across the open battlefield. I would cower in fear while I waited for the signal to deploy, but I wanted to be included with my brothers so I was willing to make the sacrifice.

A few days into our battle, Sandy decided that our younger team needed a bit more of an advantage, as we were getting the worst of it. The way things were going, the fight would last about an hour or more, and then, as if on some unknown cue, there would be a truce until the next agreed-upon day to fight. Another battle would happen in three days, as some of the guys from Robin's army had part-time jobs or wanted to check out some girls in town.

So to give us an advantage, Sandy devised a most ingenious but deadly weapon, one that to this day gives me the shud-ders to think of. Situated across the road, nearly parallel to our battleground, was my Uncle Edward's lot. He had cut back an ancient apple tree and left a perfect Y shape in its crotch. Each limb was about fifteen centimetres across. Sandy went to search through our dad's shop, where all manner of repairs were done on vehicles and heavy equipment.

I tagged along, not knowing what Sandy was planning. After looking around for a few minutes, he reached down, saying to himself more than me, "This will be perfect!" Pulling an old logging truck inner tube out of a waste barrel, he proceeded to cut it into one continuous strip of rubber, half a metre wide and two and a half metres long. Once it was cut, we headed over to the apple tree. As we approached, I started to understand what Sandy was about to build. He wrapped the tube around the limbs on each side of the Y above the centre of the crotch, then nailed the inner tube to the tree until he was satisfied it would stay firmly in place.

While putting the finishing touches on his giant slingshot, Sandy instructed me to look for some rocks, the rounder the better and at least as big as softballs. I wandered along the ditch by the road and near where Mom had tried to grow a garden. There were too many rocks for a good garden, but they were exactly what Sandy wanted for his slingshot. I gathered twenty-five to thirty rocks, filling my red wagon, or rather my and Terry's wagon, twice. We had a good supply ready to go. Sandy was brimming with excitement and anticipation to try out our new secret weapon. Robin and his buddies did not know of our project, nor would they until the next battle ensued.

Grabbing a rock from those I had stockpiled, Sandy placed it into the centre of the inner tube, checked that no vehicles were coming (for safety's sake), pulled back hard and let it hurl across the road toward the battlefield. Unfortunately, although it cleared Evergreen Road easily enough, it fell right in the middle of our side, not clearing the open area between Robin's side and ours. We tried a couple more times, and by changing the trajectory and using slightly smaller rocks we could almost reach the open area. Which still would not be sufficient.

We sat by the tree for a few minutes trying to figure how we would be able to get enough distance on the slingshot. Suddenly, Sandy jumped to his feet and ran back to Dad's shop. Grabbing some chunks of the firewood that Dad used to heat the shop, Sandy split them until they were five to eight centimetres thick. With a sledgehammer and the axe, we headed back to the tree.

Sandy used the axe to make crude points on one end of each stick—about two dozen of them—then pounded them into the ground, starting at the farthest point he'd been able to pull the slingshot back without being overpowered by its tautness. He placed the stakes at a slight angle away from the tree in a pattern that would allow him to use each as a brace to gain more leverage as he pulled back on the slingshot. After he had finished, he ran back to the shop, grabbed a thick chunk of rope and returned with new enthusiasm.

He had not said anything to me of what he was planning, so I was pretty confused until he handed me the rope. After tying a large eye loop into my end, he wrapped the rope around his hips. He picked up another big stone, loaded it and pulled back on the sling, telling me to also pull him hard as he went back. Now I knew what his plan for me was—as he stepped back to brace against each stake, I would add extra leverage by pulling on the rope around his hips as far back as I could go. Then I would hold him there until he was ready to launch the boulder.

I got as low as I could, and just like in tug-of-war, I began to pull. Sandy was able to move back several more steps before I could go no farther. But he yelled for me to hold on as he made sure no cars were coming. Assured it was safe, he let the rock fly—and fly it did. We had gained an exponential increase in fire power. The boulder flew high through the air, easily clearing the open area between our side and Robin's. After we went to investigate how far it had gone, we found it was more than twelve metres into the area that Robin and his team would be in. Success! We were now going to tip the scales of war far in our favour.

The morning came for the battle, once more, to begin. Flags were raised and arrows and spears again filled the skies. After only a few minutes Sandy and I fell back to the secret weapon. One of the other young kids on our side was to report whether we were on target or not, then Sandy would make the required changes in the trajectory and windage to wreak havoc on those below.

We were locked and loaded, the road clear. *Fire!* Off went the first boulder missile. Moments later, we got the signal that we were just a little short of the target. We reloaded, made the adjustment and fired again, this time getting an OK sign that we were on the mark. We continued the air bombardment until we had exhausted our supply arsenal and my energy. We went back to the battle front to continue in traditional warfare, until we again called a bilateral truce.

It was by the grace of God that nobody was killed or seriously injured, although there were some extremely close calls. I believe Sandy and Robin must have discussed the dangers further because in the next battle we no longer used our fantastic weapon of war. The last battle of the summer took place in early August, after a couple of days of rain and wind. As always, I took up my position behind the barricade and continued to retrieve spent weapons. Not long into the battle and on the cue to get more fallen spears and arrows, I took a quick peek out at the field. It looked quiet enough. I stood fully erect and just as I was about to jump clear of the guard, *thwack*—an arrow found its mark smack in the corner of my right eye. It lodged itself in tight between my orbital bone and my eyeball—an arm's length of polished branch dangling out of my eye. I stood there dumbfounded, not knowing what to do.

I was quickly surrounded on both sides. My brother Robin held my shoulder and hustled me toward home, saying to me, "Just tell Dad you tripped and fell on the stick." Both he and Sandy were terrified to remove the arrow, thinking that it might pull out my eyeball completely, like a marshmallow on a stick. I assured my brothers I wouldn't tell Dad.

As we crossed Evergreen Road, just before entering our yard, the arrow fell out and blood began to trickle down my right cheek. When we neared the house, Dad came out to see why there were twelve kids running up to the house all at once.

I burst into tears as soon as I saw my dad and spilled my guts like a gangster ratting out his crime family. "Dad!" I cried. "They shot an arrow in my eye!" I bawled my head off, but Dad was not impressed in the slightest and gave my older brothers a logger-style tongue lashing.

Fortunately, there was no lasting effect of the arrow to my eye. It healed quicker than the anger of our father. But that would be the end of the Evergreen War, at least fought that way!

* * *

Footnote to this story: My brothers and a couple of their buddies were down on the lot one afternoon, right before school would be starting. I'm not sure why they were there. Suddenly, just as fast as the time I took the arrow, they again were running up the road to our property, this time yelling, "They're after us!" Again my Dad was home, and we could hear them yelling from in the house. Dad ran out as they all converged at the garage, pointing back at two men running up to the house and yelling, "There they are! They're trying to get us!"

After one of these dangerous men finished tying his shoelace at the bottom of the yard, he joined his friend at the garage. My dad said, "What the hell do you want?" To which one of the men, still breathing hard and visibly pissed, replied, "These bloody kids have cut all the trees down on our property, and who the hell is going to pay?"

My poor dad agreed to pay damages and the men agreed not to have the older kids, including Sandy and Robin, charged. I believe it cost Dad one thousand dollars. In 1964 that was a lot of money—in fact, it is still a good chunk of cash now!

Free Wheelin' Three Wheelin'

Do you know how long it takes to hacksaw the roof off a 1952 Volkswagen Beetle? I know exactly how long: two days. Back in 1970 I picked up a classic Beetle before it became a classic— for fifty bucks. What a deal.

Spring in Kelowna was beautiful and warm, with all kinds of great places to go bombing around on the myriad of gravel roads throughout the Okanagan Valley. Back in those good old days I liked to go up into Gallagher's Canyon, just southeast of Kelowna, in the hills above town. I was only fourteen, but nothing was going to stop me from driving without a licence. The key was to not get caught.

The vw was a hot little rig and kind of claustrophobic for me, so one day I decided to make me a dune buggy, and of course dune buggies have no roofs. Two days and about six hacksaw blades later, I accomplished the task. I couldn't afford a roll bar, unfortunately, but at least I would be able to feel the air whistling past me as I sped down the roads that were favourite haunts of mine.

I got up early the next day, not long after daybreak, when the roads would be a bit quieter and cops were less likely to be out. Remember, I had no licence to drive so I needed to be somewhat cautious. I must have been blessed because I drove for three years without one, driving five different vehicles, and

I never got stopped once.

Some of the kids used to go up to the canyon to party, and they'd found some nice off-road areas to drive. Heading up to Rutland on the Black Mountain Road, I turned off to take some back roads out through the Southeast Kelowna area. Still keeping a low profile from police detection, I arrived at my planned destination. There was no one anywhere to be seen. I had the hills and fields to myself. It was midweek, so that would explain it—it was a pretty secluded area back then. Now it is becoming very built up. Orchards were removed and more subdivisions have replaced the farms and rural setting that existed nearly fifty years ago.

I had a blast bombing around the hills in my homemade buggy. It might not have been a 4x4, but I could take that little beast almost anywhere. After a couple of fun-filled hours, I checked my fuel gauge and realized I was getting close to empty. Deciding it was time to head back home, I cut through some forested area that was fairly open until I came back onto the canyon road.

There weren't too many straight stretches along the road, but as I was bombing down a fairly good one I hit a little pothole. A moment later I saw, off to my left, a wheel go rolling past me. Bewildered at what I had just witnessed, I could not think of a reasonable explanation for it until I looked back at my left rear wheel—at least where it was supposed to be. I realized that the wheel now pulling ahead of me was mine!

Unsure of what to do next, I did the only reasonable thing I could do: nothing. Careening down the gravel road at sixty-five km/h, I would soon run out of straight stretch. I slowed to fifty and the vw started to dip on the driver's side. Meanwhile the tire, as if in a rut, kept running straight down the road until, about sixty metres ahead of me, it crashed into the ditch on the right-hand side.

I knew I had to stop before the right turn required at the end of the straight section of the road or, when I turned, it would be over for me and my little buggy. The left side had no ditch, only a sharp drop-off to the canyon below.

When I slammed on the brakes, the vw dropped onto the left rear wheel and I spun a five-forty and came to a sudden stop facing back where I had come from. I ran up the road to where my wheel had finally stopped, brought it back to my car, removed one stud from each of the other wheels, bolted it on and was back on my way, no worse for wear.

That little bug brought me a lot of fun until it finally gave up. I left it where it died on the side of a road just outside of Rutland, for whoever decided they wanted it. With no registration it would never be traced to me. When I bought it, I had simply given the fellow $50, taken his keys and driven it away.

Boy, I sure do miss those days. Yee-haw!

Got a Light?

Summer of '69 was waning and soon we would be back in school. The routine of everyday life would begin and another year would plod along until summer holidays were here again. A couple buddies and I were thinking of things we could do during these last few days of glorious freedom.

One of my buddies, Tim, had horses. He suggested we could see if his dad would let us take them for an overnight camping/fishing trip up to a small lake we called Trapper Lake, situated about an hour and a half northeast of Rutland on horseback. His dad agreed and the plans were finalized; all the food, gear and equipment required were readied for the trip.

Early the next day, we met at Tim's place. Tim pretty much had the horses saddled and ready to go. The morning was clear but a little chilly; however, it was going to be a glorious last day of August. We shouldered our packs, climbed aboard our trusty steeds and were on our way.

Halfway up to the lake we were relentlessly attacked by horseflies. Actually, in keeping with their name, the horseflies were intent on pestering our poor mounts, who shook, shuddered and swished their tails constantly. They even took the odd jolt forward to be shed of the unwanted pests. Of course, straddling these walking bait traps, we began to serve as a satisfactory alternative to horse flesh. The flies tormented us until we finally arrived at the lake.

We put the horses into a makeshift corral that was already up at the lake. Then we took our packs into what was left of an old log cabin, basically a shell with a broken-down roof that offered the occupants the opportunity to enjoy the starlit nights. We did a little fishing from shore, caught nothing, but we were happy just to be away from everyone at home, camping and enjoying hot dogs roasted over our campfire. We did some exploring for the rest of the day and then, as the sun began to dip below the horizon, decided to head into the log shell where our camp was set up.

We got the fire going again. It was safe, even as we stirred the fire and added more chunks of dead wood, because the smoke and sparks floated out the nearly non-existent roof. With our supper finished and the stories soon to start, we could now lie back and enjoy a smoke and a favourite pop from the batch we were keeping cold in the lake.

We all looked around the room waiting for someone to pull out a pack of smokes. "Okay, who brought the smokes?" The three of us spoke almost simultaneously, looking eagerly at each other. "I didn't. I thought you did," was the common answer. No one in particular had been given the responsibility to bring them so we'd all assumed the others would.

This was a terrible state of affairs. Camping at the lake all by ourselves, no rules, a good campfire, delicious roasted hot dogs, cold pop—but no smokes. We sat there angrily blaming each other, when suddenly a thought came to me.

All around the cabin, inside and out, were copious amounts of pine needles. They were bone dry and we had newspapers for fire starter. I continued to formulate my plan, unbeknownst to my two buddies. I gathered up a pot full of pine needles, laid a small row across a piece of newspaper, then, as tightly as I could, I rolled them into the biggest joint this side of Jamaica. It would have made any Rasta proud.

Once my pals saw what I was doing, they figured it out. Holding the joint like I was playing clarinet, I leaned into the fire and took a long pull. Within a split second a large volume of pine-scented, acrid smoke entered my lungs. Still holding this gigantic home-rolled smoke, I barked and coughed at least half of one lung out. My head reeled with extreme dizziness, my throat burned and my eyes watered... it had worked perfectly! My pals, not to be left out of this extraordinary experience, lined up to take their respective pulls, with the same effect on them as it had on me.

So you're thinking, "That was very stupid," and of course it would be natural for you to think the three of us would feel the same. No such thing—we kept passing that mega-joint around until we were so ill and dizzy that we could barely stand. I took the last drag before dumping the remainder of the joint into the fire.

We collapsed onto our sleeping bags, on the verge of tossing up the hot dogs and marshmallows of only a couple hours earlier. Finally, stomachs settling down, heads a little clearer, we began to brag about how clever we were. Necessity is truly the mother of invention. We finally decided we needed an appropriate name for our ingenious invention. Names like Super Joint, the Big Stick, Joker Smoker and a few more I can't recall were suggested. After all our possible names were played out, we unanimously agreed on one name that was the most identifiable: the Pineola. It had a nice ring and would look good on a cigarette package.

We never tried such an experiment again, thank goodness. It will always remain in my journal entry as probably the stupidest thing I ever did. And take my word for it, I have done plenty of stupid things in my lifetime.

"Pineolas, with that cool menthol taste." We could have made a fortune!

He's Not Dead!

Looks like I'm bear hunting by myself today. Bob can't make it as planned, but I'm not sitting at home on a perfect bear-hunting day in late August.

It was 1977 and Bob and I had made plans to go to Bacon Lake up near Strathcona Park. I was fine with heading up on my own, as it was one of my favourite times of the year.

The logging slashes were at least fifteen years old and lush with fireweed, huckleberry and blueberry bushes. The giant blue grouse that called this area home would be a great side catch if the bear were not co-operating. It was still archery season and I was using my fifty-two pound Ben Pearson Recurve, which already had one bear to its credit.

Crossing the Strathcona Dam, I turned left and headed up northeast of Becher Lake. Once I entered the first open slash, I parked off to the side and continued on up the old logging road on foot. The road was becoming more deeply rutted as heavy West Coast rains pounded the hillsides with flash floods; finding the easiest way down, the rain usually ended up washing out the road. I didn't mind the road erosion too much, as it certainly kept the road hunters out of the area, except for those 4×4 enthusiasts who loved a challenge.

I had walked less than fifty metres when I noticed a large fresh pile of bear scat on the road. It wasn't warm but

I could tell that it had been deposited within the last hour or so.

I placed an arrow on the arrow-rest of my Recurve and slowed my pace. I took four or five steps, looked in all directions for a few seconds before carrying on, then proceeded in this "still hunt" style. Rounding a corner where some large trees stood next to a sloping rock bluff, I caught some movement. Turning slowly so I would be directly facing the spot where I had seen the movement, I saw a good-sized black bear that had climbed up onto a very large windfall.

Bears loved to rip these old trees apart for the grubs living inside the disintegrating wood. With it standing broadside to me at a distance of less than ten metres, I wasn't entirely sure it was a shot I wanted to take. But that thought was short-lived. I came to full draw then let the arrow fly. *Thuck!* The arrow struck its mark into the bear's lungs.

The bear took one bound along the log then flipped sideways off the giant deadfall. I waited, hearing only a little movement at first, then after five minutes all was quiet. I climbed up onto the log, where minutes earlier the bear had stood. I could barely get up onto the tree—it was well over a metre in diameter and about thirty centimetres off the ground, just sitting in the shin-tangle. I found another spot farther down the log where I could climb up more easily.

Scrambling back up to where the bear had fallen, I could see him—it was a young boar—lying on his side wedged between the log and the rock slope it was up against. Feeling confident he was dead, I jumped down behind him. I set my bow down behind me so it wouldn't be in the way in my confined space and pulled out my ten-centimetre lock-back knife to begin the gutting. I grabbed the left rear leg to flip the bear onto its back for dressing, and pulled him over, only to find that he was not even close to being dead!

He let out a moaning growl, striking back at me with his left front paw and simultaneously pulling a hind leg under him as if trying to turn to face me. Still wedged between the rock face and the log, he struggled mightily. Still, I was sure he was mortally hit—at least I was hoping he was. I reached back, feeling for my bow, not daring to take my eyes off the bear for fear he would turn at that very second and be upon me.

Finding the bow, I nocked another arrow, went to full draw and waited. The bear continued his struggle to turn himself to face me. I felt the urge to shoot him again for a neck shot, then decided that the pain of a second shot might only give him the impetus to complete his turn. I was afraid to turn to the log and try to climb back over the slippery, rotting obstacle because I would have to release the draw. I kept holding the full draw until my shoulder and arms began to shake. At last, unable to hold it any longer, I released it for a second then again drew the bow back.

Then there was the slow moving of limbs and the relaxing of the bear's body, so I now knew he had finally succumbed to his wound. I poked with the broadhead on my arrow hard into his rump; no response. I continued to prod the bear until I could finally touch his eyeball. There was no response. I sat down to calm my nerves and give my fatigued arms and shoulders a break.

The unique thing about archery hunting is the challenge of being able to stalk close enough to your prey to make a clean kill. However, when bow-hunting bears, ten metres is as close as I ever want to get.

Next time I might just pass up the shot!

Hooked a Beauty!

"Sure, I can take you out for a charter. No problem using your own boat. I'll just charge for my time. See you tomorrow morning at the Tyee Spit boat launch in Campbell River. Be there by 5:00 in the morning." After I hung up the phone, I went through my fishing gear to make sure I had everything in order for first thing the next morning.

I had begun working as a fishing guide in 1973, shortly after I moved to Vancouver Island from Rutland, and just months after marrying my first wife, Lynne. I kind of learned as I went, and over the years I'd personally caught fifteen tyee and helped many others catch limits of coho and many tyee. Now, seven years later, I felt confident of my ability to charter on my own.

My clients were already up in Courtenay on Vancouver Island. They had been given my name and number by a client I had taken out on a charter the previous year. We'd caught some nice springs, one of which was over eighteen kilos, so these new folks were feeling optimistic about their chances.

It was late in August but there were still some spring salmon being taken. It was slowing down, though. The Campbell River, where they were milling at the mouth and near the estuary, was a little higher than normal from some rains that had fallen during our wetter than normal August. Water authorities were letting a little more flow out from the John Hart Dam upriver so the salmon were already starting to make their way up the river. Some northern coho were starting to show up in front of Dolphins Resort, just north of Orange Point, which was near the Elk Falls Mill. We would probably target the northern coho and still have a chance of picking up a late-season spring salmon.

I arrived around 4:45 a.m. and was taking all my rods and tackle to the boat launch in preparation to load when my clients arrived. Right on time, they pulled up in front of the launch with their seventeen-foot boat.

I was the only person there, so they safely assumed that I was indeed Kelly, their guide. Their names elude me after all this time, so I will call them Tom, Dave and Dave's very attractive wife, Jill. They were in their mid-twenties, friendly and ready to go fishing.

After making our introductions and a bit of small talk, I loaded my gear into the boat, which was still on the boat trailer. I laid my two Fenwick trolling rods across one of the seats, as they were too long to lay anywhere else. Next, I gave instructions to Tom and Jill to be very careful getting into the boat. I did not want them to step on my rods or sit on them. They were expensive and were already rigged with bucktails and double-hook setups. "No problem, we'll be careful," they said.

Dave and I would launch the boat after Tom and Jill were aboard to make it easier, as there was no dock to walk out on after we launched. I would have to jump on last, with probably wet feet for my efforts.

Tom, being a gentleman, waved his hand forward to the boat and motioned for Jill to get on first. As daylight was a half-hour away and it was still fairly dark, I cautioned Jill again to please not step on my fishing rods. She replied, "I won't, I'll be careful." She swung her free leg over the side of the boat, then promptly sat herself down on my rods.

There was a short squeal of pain, so I knew we had a problem. "What happened?" Dave asked. A moment of silence, then the very timid answer came forth: "I just sat on a fishing rod, and something sharp is poked into me." Dave said, "Well, get off his rod and sit on the other seat." "I can't," was Jill's response. "I think I have a hook stuck in me and you need to get it out."

The three of us stood there, not sure how to respond until Jill asked Dave again, "Can you please pull the hook out?" Clearly a little frustrated—this was cutting into our valuable fishing time—Dave asked her where the hook was stuck.

"I just told you—by my private area!"

Tom instantly suggested we call an ambulance, but Jill vehemently objected to that idea. Dave agreed with her. I told him that if we wanted to go fishing he needed to get the hook out—now! He looked at me with a fearful you've-got-to-be-kidding expression and defaulted to his friend Tom, who likewise said, "No chance I'm doing that." As the two argued back and forth, Jill finally had enough. "Will someone *please* get the hook out of me?!"

Dave turned to me with the look of a lost child. "Could you please take out the hook? You should be very experienced at doing that kind of thing." Never one to turn down a challenge, and wanting to get fishing so I could get paid, I somewhat reluctantly agreed.

By now it was getting light enough to see the oncoming day on the horizon. Using the penlight I kept in my tackle box, I climbed up into the boat. Loosening the drag on the rod, I gave Jill enough slack to turn around to face the seat and give me a clear shot at her lower backside and the situation at hand. Positioning myself behind her, I still could not see the hook clearly—I needed her to arch her back more and push her behind out toward me, which she did without hesitation.

I could now see the 4.0 hook impaled into what I realized was a very sensitive area. Jill never even winced as I reached up to extract the hook. Just as I began the removal, a couple in their mid-forties backed down the ramp to launch their boat. The woman got out to remove the boat straps. She slowly walked past us, staring with disdain and disbelief. We all greeted her with a "Good morning and good luck."

I could only imagine what was going on in this woman's mind, as she obviously did not have all the information she needed to make a sound judgment about what she was seeing. Her look told me that we definitely needed to get a room or a priest!

I continued to wiggle the hook until I could see the point of it and its barb sticking out from Jill's jeans. I have to say it was the first time in my life, and probably ever, that I was touching a beautiful lady's womanhood with her husband and a friend paying rapt attention. I removed the hook and took a cold shower. (Okay, I didn't do that, but I probably should have.)

Finally, we launched the boat and ended up having a great day's fishing, landing some nice northern coho. I got paid for my fishing services. However, I sadly received no payment for medical services rendered, considering how difficult they had been for me, a full-blooded twenty-two-year-old man. It had taken a determined effort for me to stay focused during the hook extraction—and, for that matter, to keep my mind on any normal tasks for the next few days!

Howe Island Swimming Lesson

When I was a young child, our family spent time living in float camps around the coastal areas of British Columbia. My mother, Rose, had her hands full trying to keep any of us from drowning in the murky depths of the cold coastal inlets that were home for us. I was nearly five years old when we moved out to yet another camp where Dad and Ernie Alexander, a family friend, were logging.

Howe Island was, for a change, a camp situated on land. It consisted of a few houses on float logs, skidded up onto the beach above the high-water mark. My mother was not there yet—she was still home with my two younger sisters, Penny and Debbie, and my youngest brother Leslie. She was to come on the last trip to camp. This trip it was Terry and me going with Dad. Robin and Sandy had made the trip out to the camp earlier with Dad and Ernie.

Soon we were pulling into a little bay where the camp was located. Dad pulled up beside the dock, tied the boat up and told Terry and me to hop out. He motioned for us, still wearing our bulky old life jackets, to start heading down the dock toward shore, twenty-five metres or so away.

We had just started to walk down the dock when suddenly I felt myself being lifted into the air by the straps on my life jacket. Terry, likewise, was hanging from his straps. Dad turned to the edge of the dock and then, without warning, tossed us both into the freezing ocean. "If you're going to live by the water you might as well learn to swim," he declared matter-of-factly.

Panicked and shocked by the cold water, I flailed helplessly as I watched my father stride away, never looking back. I hollered and sputtered as my splashing sent waves of water into my face; I was half breathing and half drinking the salty brine. Terry, who was three years older, quickly figured out what he needed to do. As he pulled away from me and swam toward shore, my panic kicked into a higher gear and I flailed even harder. Terry was over halfway to shore, leaving me to be eaten by whatever denizens of the deep were there just waiting to pull me down. They surely must have heard the commotion by now.

I stared at the shore, a few tears finding their way down my cheeks to mix with the salt water dripping from my head. Dad was now out of sight. Out of abject fear and the desire to be with him on shore, I began to heave myself forward, as if pulling on an imaginary rope that would bring me home.

That simple action moved me in Terry's direction—he was now walking out of the water and onto the beach. I continued to pull myself forward. Finally, after a few terrifying minutes, I reached the shore, and victory! Even if no one, including my dad, showed pride in my success at making it to shore, at least I was very happy.

I have had a fear of the ocean ever since. It's ironic that someone like me, who is so afraid of the ocean, has spent so many hours on it.

It's Money All the Same

Working as a fishing guide was full of unique and exciting adventures. However, they were not always the kind you would expect to have while enjoying a day of fishing. You were expected to babysit grown men and women, be a tour guide on all things historical, know how to perform CPR, have basic mechanical skills, be well versed on tidal currents, read weather patterns quickly, catch copious numbers of fish, of course, and for the most part know everything about anything. Then there are those days that you simply have no answer for what happens on your boat. This is one of those particular days.

Fishing had been slow for at least two weeks, and action was spotty at best for a few days with fairly weak tides, and what salmon were cruising the Johnstone Strait near Campbell River were few and far between. I had returned from a morning charter with three folks from Los Angeles. We were fortunate to pick up three decent coho out at the Red Can—a marker buoy identifying a reef that jutted out south of Quadra Island, which at low tide would have less than a metre of water covering the boulder-strewn bottom. We arrived back at 11:00 a.m. I unloaded the fourteen-foot fibreglass open runabout, cleaned my party's fish, accepted a small gratuity and wished them a good day. I had no other charters lined up for the afternoon until 4:00 p.m. so I grabbed a burger from A&W then went back to my boat for a pleasant siesta in the late July sun.

I had no sooner nodded off when Dave, the charter operator, came over and woke me up. "Do you want to take a party out?"

I told Dave, "The fishing will be dead but if they want to go that bad, I guess I can. It's money all the same."

As I completed preparing the boat with life jackets, new full fuel tanks and gear, a short, well-dressed man came walking down the dock. He looked to be in his early thirties. Accompanying him was a very good-looking lady in her mid-twenties, well endowed and dressed equally uptown, wearing a rather short miniskirt and heels.

These two can't be my charter, can they? I thought. I stood by the little dock house where Dave's office was and surmised, *They must just be tourists out for a stroll on the dock.* I was wrong. The little fellow walked up to me and without a thought for the consequence said, "Hey boy, you gonna catch us a big one?"

That didn't sit well with me. "First let's get this straight," I replied. "I am not your boy." I may have been only eighteen but if someone can rip your head off in a heartbeat it is wise not to call him "boy"!

He gave a half-hearted apology, introduced himself and his companion and again asked if fishing would be good. I told him, "Honestly, I don't think it will be that great. We have a lousy tide and it's been quite quiet." Out of the corner of my eye, I could see Dave frowning at me with a stern be-quiet look. It's money all the same, right?

With little enthusiasm I helped them into the boat, went over a couple of concerns about safe boating etiquette and remarked that they weren't really dressed for fishing. "We're fine, no problem," the man said. We pushed off from the dock and headed over to Tyee Pool, just south of the Campbell River. I felt there might be a chance of picking up an early chinook or spring salmon preparing to head up the Campbell River in a few weeks or so.

Whenever I was using jigs such as Buzz Bombs or Stingsildas, two popular jigging lures I had good success with, I would fish over the stern of the boat as well. We would be fishing right near the bottom and my clients would fish over each side of the boat. Fishing this way, I could use my line position in the water to keep their lines straight down. If my line was straight, so was theirs. I would use the motor to manoeuvre the boat by putting the stern against the tide then reversing every so often so as not to allow the boat to drift faster than the lines.

This style didn't allow for much eye contact, but we could still communicate quite well, even though my back was facing them most of the time. I got my rod out first, then turned to put out their rods, to which the little man said, "No, we're fine. You go ahead and fish for us." *What a strange dude*, I thought, *but what the heck, I'm getting paid all the same.*

Fifteen minutes went slowly by; no hits. I just kept drifting and jigging, basically wasting the day. We had not seen anyone else on the water except a passing cruise ship in the middle of the channel. While I fished I could hear the two of them laughing quietly, with the young woman sometimes making strange sounds. Maybe not really strange in general, but strange for fishing.

Just as I was about to reel up my line and move the boat up for another drift, *wham!* I hit a good fish. It started to take a good run, peeling off about eighteen metres of line. I hollered back to my clients, "I have a nice spring on. Who wants it?" There was no response. Not taking my eyes off the fighting spring, which was on the surface and about forty-five metres away, I shouted again, "Who wants this fish?"

Still no response. Frustrated, I turned to see why they were not answering me. What I saw next was an image that would be hard to erase from my mind. They had piled up the life jackets against the bow of the boat. He had her dress hiked up far past her hips, with no underwear visible and her breasts also exposed.

Dumbfounded, I stared for a few moments while she smiled at me with a kind of come-hither look. His back was still turned to me but positioned to make sure I had an unobstructed view.

Finally, returning to the situation at hand, I focused on the fish, which was still on. I reeled in my spring and, trying not to make eye contact, said, "We're going back in now." The fellow said, "I thought it was a three-hour minimum?" "No, not anymore it isn't!" I said emphatically.

A couple of hours after we returned I replayed the whole story to Dave. Shaking his head in disbelief, he told me that he'd charged for three hours anyway, which the fellow never complained about.

Back then, as a worldly teenager, the thought of how I could have better handled this situation briefly passed through my thoughts. It involved me throwing the guy overboard and… well, you get the picture. After all, it's money all the same!

A Lion and a Bear

As you may have gathered, I am an enthusiastic bear hunter. I enjoy the hunt experience. I love the meat as well as the beautiful, luxurious late fall or early spring hide. I had longed to do a spring grizzly hunt up to the head of Knight Inlet, where the Klinaklini River enters the mouth of the inlet, and I finally got the chance in the spring of 1979. Being early May, this would coincide with the annual eulachon run. These small, oily fish would soon fill the water from shore to shore as they entered the river to spawn.

The trees on either bank were lined with hundreds of bald eagles, gorging on the spent and spawning eulachons. When we arrived they were already beginning to abstain from eating any more of these very rich fish. The fish were even more oily than the eagles could handle after a few days of feasting.

My hunting companion would be a fellow named Gord. We left Campbell River shortly after 10:00 on a Thursday morning. Our transportation was a twenty-four-foot Reinell Cuddy that would serve as our hunting camp. Arriving near the mouth of the inlet in the late afternoon, we decided to stay the night at an old logging dock around the corner from the Klinaklini Valley's estuary.

Not long after we settled in for supper, we heard a roaring sound echoing off the surrounding mountains that rose steeply above the inlet. The sheer walls reached six to nine hundred metres above the cold, dark waters of Knight Inlet. Curious about what was making such a ruckus, we untied the boat from its mooring and headed around the point.

As soon as we entered the final turn in the inlet, we saw two Indigenous fellows in a rickety old tin boat. They were racing around the bay shooting at something. When we were within seventy-five metres of them, we could now see what they were shooting at: huge sea lions. The roaring we'd heard was the animals' barking, almost a lion-like roar, hence the name sea lion.

We pulled up alongside the two guys and asked what they were doing, mostly as a way of starting a conversation. It was obvious to us what they were doing. One of the men, Paddy, said they were trying to shoot a sea lion. I later learned that they used the whiskers for ceremonial purposes.

Looking down at their well-abused .303 British army rifle, I was not surprised that they kept missing. What was surprising was that the rusty, antiquated rifle didn't blow up in their faces! After they answered us, they asked Gord and me the same question. We explained that we had come up to hunt grizzly bears and we were going up the river to do so. Paddy, seeing my .30-06 sitting on the motor housing, commented, "I bet that gun could sure shoot a sea lion easy." I nodded, agreeing that it could.

He then eagerly asked me, like a child wanting another cookie, if I would shoot one for him and his brother, Herb. When I happily agreed, he instructed me to shoot for the head. "That way it'll stay afloat and can be towed to shore. If you shoot it in the body it will sink." Again I agreed that indeed, I would do that. Pointing out a suitable large male, he excitedly hollered, "That one over near the river mouth!"

Spotting the lion at nearly one hundred metres, I rested my rifle on the gunwale of the boat, took a couple of breaths, exhaled slowly, then, holding my breath to be steady, fired. A perfect hit! The lion rolled a bit to one side then lay there motionless. Paddy whooped. "Holy cow, nice shot!" I felt like I had just broken one of my rules about shooting something for no reason other than what I thought was a frivolous thing—the long, extremely hard whiskers that protruded from its jaw. The two men thanked me profusely.

Herb Joseph, Paddy's brother, who was also the chief of what was then known as the Alert Bay Indian Band, asked us to be his guests and stay up the river mouth at their eulachon camp. We graciously accepted, as we would be going upriver in the morning anyway. We towed the sea lion up the river to where we could get it onto the beach. Beaching it took the better part of a day because it was nearly high tide and the river was affected by the tide in the estuary. Also, to try and salvage some reason for killing the magnificent mammal, I decided that I would at least skin it out. If I had only known how much work it would be, I might have opted for the guilty conscience.

After towing in the lion and tying it as high up the riverbank as possible, we docked the boat. The smell of hundreds of thousands of rotting eulachons piled ten centimetres deep on the beach above the high water mark was absolutely horrific. The band had constructed two large rectangular cauldrons to render down the putrefying fish. So as to be able to get all the oil out of the little grease sticks, they simmered these fish for hours. Once this was done, they siphoned off the rich oil into gallon jugs. Eulachon grease, a vitamin-rich cooking grease, is a valuable delicacy among the coastal First Nations. In 1979 a gallon of clear was worth $100 and the opaque or unclear, which was a lesser grade, could fetch $75 or more.

As nightfall came and after visiting for a while with Herb and Paddy, we called it a day and headed to bed. Sometime in the early morning I awoke suddenly. It was still quite dark out. The boat was listing heavily to the port side at nearly a forty-five-degree angle. I could feel the river buffeting the underside of the hull.

I shook Gord awake, who had somehow slept soundly through it all, and we grabbed a flashlight and staggered awkwardly to the deck. We were beached in the river, as the tide had receded. But how the hell had we drifted down the river to start with? A little investigation soon revealed how: our bow line had been cut and we were set adrift.

Apparently, not everyone was happy about us being on reserve land.

When the tide began to come back in, Gord jumped into the water and pushed the boat while I pushed off the bottom with a paddle. Once we got enough water under the keel we checked for any out-drive damage. It looked okay so we fired up the boat, went back to the dock at the eulachon camp and retied the boat. This time with a much smaller bow line than we originally had.

Herb was furious. He seemed to know who the culprits were because it never happened again. Then, maybe feeling bad for what had happened or just because he was a good man, he offered us a little aluminum boat with a 9.8 HP outboard motor to go up the river to where we were planning to hunt. We gladly accepted his offer.

First light the next morning, we were on our way up the Klinaklini. I had brought my .30-06, but being a keen bow hunter I'd also brought my sixty-pound compound bow with the hope that I might kill my first grizzly with a bow. After we arrived upriver at a place where the river branched off then joined again farther upstream, Gord dropped me off on the rocky beach where the river bottom widened. By splitting up, we would cover more area and double our chances of finding a shootable grizzly bear. The river continued on up the valley for couple of kilometres or so, treed in aspen and poplar, with the odd river-bottom spruce struggling among the overabundant hardwoods.

After I gave Gord the thumbs-up sign, he waved back and carried on up the river, following the main channel. I slung my rifle over my shoulder and nocked an arrow in my bow, determined that I was going to shoot my first grizzly with this primitive weapon. I had taken three black bears with archery gear, but never a grizzly.

I have made some dumb decisions in my life, however. In retrospect, I now know this was more than likely the stupidest thing I have ever done. I thought if I had my rifle handy I could use it in an emergency to bail me out if things went horribly wrong. In reality, I would never be able to shoulder my rifle in enough time to be able to back myself up!

Not long after I entered the bush, I began to feel a little uneasy and kept up a running internal battle between leaving my bow on the trail and continuing on with only my rifle or taking them both. The desire to accomplish the feat with my bow, and my machismo, won out. I carried on with both. Twenty minutes later found me deep into the timbered river bottom. I heard the snap of a branch. I stopped, listened intently, straining to pinpoint the sound. With no follow-up sound, I shrugged it off as more than likely a branch falling.

Just as I took a couple more steps, I heard another noise, like the crunch of dead and dried leaves under the foot of something. This time the sound was close and slightly to my right. But I could see nothing. However, that uneasy feeling began to raise my concern as well as my heart rate. This continued on for another hundred metres or so. Something was definitely following me.

The decision to shoulder my rifle was now much easier to make. My machismo was replaced by serious concern for my safety. Continuing on, I suddenly broke through into the other side of the timbered river bottom, and a little more than ten metres away lay a half-buried fresh cow moose carcass, not yet even chewed on.

I stood transfixed, staring at the half-buried animal. I began to tremble slightly, my breathing becoming more laboured, knowing now that what was following me was something big enough to down a full-grown, apparently healthy moose. I wasted no time in moving upriver from the kill. Coming to a short bluff about a hundred metres farther up the river bottom, I placed myself up on the top of the bank. It gave me a good vantage point from which to watch the grizzly kill.

Now, at a safer distance, I thought I would be able to get a shot at the bear when it came to feed on its meal. After a couple of hours, I became restless and wanted to return to the place where Gord had dropped me off a few hours earlier. We had no set time to rendezvous—Gord would either wait until I arrived back or I would wait for him, whoever got there first.

Climbing down from my vantage point, I began to head back the only way out, past the grizzly kill and through the bush. For a moment I even entertained the idea of trying to go around the treed area, but that would have meant scrambling through the rock-strewn river in icy, waist-deep glacier water. That idea was quickly dismissed. With one misstep I would more than likely drown in the ice-cold, rolling river!

As I neared the dead and buried moose, I became fearful of what could possibly be waiting for me. I knew there was a grizzly between me and the pickup point six hundred metres through this gauntlet.

Keeping as wide a berth from the grizzly kill as I could, I entered the bush. My senses were on high alert, listening for any sound other than mine. I strained to hear and to look through the trees and brush that surrounded me for any movement or shape that looked out of place.

Much like the first time through, I heard the noise of breaking branches and something moving alongside of me, stopping when I stopped then moving when I moved. Removing the safety, I held my rifle out in front of me at the ready and continued on. Finally, about forty minutes later, I reached the river. I followed it in the direction Gord had taken to be as far from the grizzly kill as possible, knowing the bear would still have to pass me at some point. I stopped to take a break and was eating a granola bar from my pack when I heard the little motor of Herb's boat. Gord appeared moments later.

The next day I went back, no bow this time. I was locked and loaded for bear but the grizzly had apparently had enough of my presence. As I retraced my steps this time, and without being too concerned about the noise I was making, I broke through at the precise spot that, only the day before, was the kill site. I found that the moose carcass had been dragged into the river. Looking across the river's small arm, I could see the telltale drag marks of the moose on the other side, about thirty metres away.

Obviously, this grizzly had felt a little crowded and decided to take its meal to a quieter place where it could eat in peace. I felt somewhat relieved. After all, I didn't think I really wanted to hunt grizzlies anymore on that trip. The day before had provided an ample adrenaline rush to keep me going for the rest of the spring grizzly season.

One Load to Go!

Ingrid and I moved our family to Kamloops in 1992. We had begun our marriage on Vancouver Island in 1987, living on York Road south of Campbell River. Before that, I had been a single father living with my two surviving sons—Brent was shot and killed at fourteen years of age—after Lynne and I had separated and prior to our divorce (that's a story I won't relate here). I was content to be single, although not completely happy. I met Ingrid on a blind date set up by two mutual friends, Tom and Cheryl Leavitt. From the moment we first met, I could not stop thinking of this beautiful woman. We phone dated, mostly, in those years before social media and texting, and we both remained celibate throughout, with no thought to marriage plans as I still lived on the Island and she lived in Surrey.

That was, until one night when she walked into a dance we were supposed to meet at. When she entered the room, everything changed: the lights went dim, the music muted and a single conduit of light connected the two of us. I gazed at her and heard a voice say to me, "This is your eternal companion." That was it—two months later we were married in Seattle at the Church of Jesus Christ of Latter-Day Saints Temple, of which we were both practising members.

After leaving Vancouver Island we moved to Lone Butte in the Cariboo region of BC. Three short years later we were in

Kamloops, where I ventured into something completely different: I began a career in real estate with HomeLife Realty. I moved down first, while Ingrid and our ever-growing family—which had started as three, my two sons and Kelly Lynn, Ingrid's daughter from a previous relationship, and then we added Samantha, Errin and Isaac—would stay at our place in Lone Butte until it sold. A couple of months later we did sell and purchased a home in Rose Hill Estates. We loved our home there but ultimately we realized it was not what we truly wanted. Nor was working in the real estate business what I wanted—some of the best people and some of the laziest and biggest liars worked in that industry. I quit after two years and decided to go logging again, on my own property.

We had moved from a large acreage, with plenty of privacy and good hunting, to living in a six-thousand-square-foot house in town. Even though we were up on Rose Hill, for all intents and purposes it *was* town. We bought and sold a few different properties until we finally found eighty-three hectares just north of Kamloops. It had timber and a kilometre of highway frontage, and it was right across from the Thompson River.

It was raw land. Our plan was to build a home there, but not for several years. We would selectively log the property, as there was some good timber, but it would take some heroic road building to gain access to the wood on the rather steep hillsides.

I had no equipment other than one chainsaw, and I'd need to find a dozer with a winch to be able to log it. I found a Cat D6 in Cache Creek that needed a new blade and some work.

However, the price was right and I had the skills to build a blade and do the mechanical work required. It was an older D6 with only a mechanical tilt for the blade, but it was at least a powershift.

I needed to secure some working capital to get things off the ground. I was introduced to a fellow by an acquaintance, Roger Ulmer. In fact, I had purchased the eighty-three hectares from Roger. Richard, Roger's associate, was willing to advance me $25,000, which would be due in three months' time. It would take fifteen loads delivered to pay the note in full, with a percentage being paid by the log broker to my lender from each load delivered.

The Cat was low-bedded out to our place in late February. We were still well into winter, and I would not be able to get up the mountain to build road for at least another month or two. I used this time to get the Cat ready to go, then do some road assessment and layout for when I could start logging the main timber up near the top of the property. It had been logged a few years earlier, but the slope was deemed too dangerous and steep to make it viable for conventional logging. I was able to harvest some smaller timber near the base of the hillside in the meantime, but that was only about two or three loads.

The weather warmed up considerably as we moved into March, and I was able to start building road. I concentrated on constructing a main spur line first, through some of the more open areas where the snow had mostly disappeared, mainly on any southwest exposures.

By April I was ready to go hardcore. I had just over one month left to fulfill my contract, so I hired my brother Lory and my nephew Trevor to help me accomplish the task. Even my brother-in-law, Trevor's dad Gary Cardno, offered to give me a hand in the beginning for a few days.

They worked hard and we started to get the wood off the hill and to the broker. We had a few close calls, but we were able to keep the dozer from falling off the mountain, where, in some places, I would be almost defying gravity to retrieve the logs. Sometimes we would have all thirty metres of our three-quarter-inch mainline out and be pulling three-eighth-inch tag lines of thirty-five to seventy metres, as some of the wood was inaccessible.

We had a series of setbacks over the remaining month but were able to keep picking away at it. It was now late May, and we had four days left to deliver the last two loads. I was falling each load of timber as we built the spurs into them and then skidding them out. I did not want to fall any trees unless I knew for sure we could actually retrieve them.

With two days left on my contract to deliver, we still had one load to go. I needed to have the last load at the log sort yard by 4:30 p.m. on May 31. If I didn't, all that I had paid already would be forfeited and the original $25,000 would still be owing as a late penalty, so there was some pressure to get it done. This need to rush may have precipitated what unfolded on the last day.

With about a third of a load, or ten cubic metres, left to go, I felt assured we would make the deadline. Lory, Trevor and I arrived out at the property around 8:00 a.m. I fired up the D6, confident we would have the remaining few logs in the landing and off to the sort yard by 3:00 p.m.

We were taking some large Douglas fir from a steep side-hill at the northwest end of my property. Those last five trees would be enough to finish the load. Just two more turns to go! We backed up the narrow skid road until I was close enough to be able to choker the first three trees we would skid down. The trees fell as planned. I bucked most of the limbs off right there. It would be easier to winch them up, and no large limbs would dig up any lurking boulders that might run down the precipitous hillside and reach the Yellowhead Highway, which was about one hundred and twenty metres below.

It was just after 10:30 a.m., and that load was safely in the landing below with my logging truck driver, Wade, who had hauled most of the wood to the sort yard in Kamloops for me. Only one more turn to go and I was home free. We returned back up the hill to fall the last few big fir that would make my fifteenth and final load. These last three trees were about forty-five centimetres in diameter and straight as power poles.

I felled all three while Trevor and Lory waited above. I laid the trees horizontal to the hill so they would be easier to limb. The first two trees were limbed with no difficulty and ready to go. Now just one more tree.

It was the lowest of the three trees on the hillside, on a very steep part of the hill, with nothing in the way to prevent it from rolling other than possibly a few old stumps from earlier logging shows. I clambered over to this big fir and began to limb it, starting from the top and working my way back to the butt. When I was nearing the end of the tree and on the downhill side, I could see only three big limbs left. My plan was to leave the last big limb in place to keep the tree from rolling, then buck it off after I had the choker on it. That was my first big mistake.

Normally, I would have put the choker on the tree first, hooked it up to the D6, then cut the last few limbs off to ensure it would not roll away on me. But I felt the last limb would be sufficient to anchor the log where it lay. Then I bucked off the second-last limb. There was a loud *crack!* The big fir broke from the remaining limb and began to careen down the hill. I jumped backwards, my feet leading the way, then fell flat onto the hill, my face wedged between two rocks.

The log kept rolling toward me. It rolled right over my head, and then from the corner of my eye I saw the butt of the tree lift high into the air. Seeing this as my opportunity to get uphill of the tree, I rose onto my hands and knees, and just as I was standing I felt the impact of a two-ton tree crashing down on my back, crushing me down to where I'd just been lying flat a moment before. It rolled over me then came to rest against an old stump on the hill just below me.

Excruciating pain shot through my spine and chest. I was rising to my knees when I suddenly experienced the most unusual thing—I could not breathe, nor did I feel much pain. I had no sensation or even any urge to breathe. It wasn't like other times, when I'd had the wind knocked out of me during years of fighting and other mishaps. I could now see only blackness. I could hear no sound except a steady hum inside my head. I had no idea how long this all lasted before I could feel sensation again. I felt Lory put his arms around me as I was still kneeling on the rocks. "Bro, you okay?" he frantically asked me over and over. I could not respond.

Then the pain returned and I felt the urge, once again, to breathe. But with Lory hugging me so intently, I could not get a breath at all. After what seemed like minutes but was probably only seconds, I was able to whisper the words, "Let go." I repeated them twice. He finally relinquished his grip and I was able to breathe again, although it was very laboured.

We stayed in that position for a few minutes until I felt I could stand. My breathing was still very difficult and I felt intense pressure on my chest. Lory half dragged me up to the dozer where Trevor was waiting. When I told him he would have to run the Cat down to the landing, he protested, "No! Not me! I'll kill us all on this steep hillside!" I could not persuade him in spite of my obvious handicap.

So I climbed into the seat and we headed down the mountain. Every pull on the steering clutches brought sharp spasms of pain through my chest and back. We reached the landing safely, loaded me into the truck and headed to Emergency at Royal Inland Hospital as fast as Lory could drive.

Lory helped me into Emergency, explaining what had just happened, and I was promptly given an X-ray—where, unbelievably, it showed I had no broken ribs. They wheeled me back to the ER, hooked me up to a monitor and gave me an oxygen mask to help me breathe.

Soon a doctor came in to see me, and he explained what had happened. Both of my lungs had collapsed and my rib cage had compressed over four centimetres. One lung had come back on its own on the hill; the other needed to have forced respiration to assist it. He was surprised that I'd been able to get to the hospital under my own steam and had no internal bleeding. The kind of trauma I had suffered, he said, would have killed almost anyone else who had been through a similar accident. He then admonished me to rest from any physical activity and especially logging for at least two or three weeks.

Smiling, he shook my hand and said, "You are a very lucky man," then walked out.

When I was first wheeled back into the ER, I told Lory to phone Ingrid and tell her I was in Emergency, but to be sure to say it was just a minor thing and I was fine. Yes, it was a lie, but I thought it was justified. Suddenly, I remembered that I had only until 4:30 to have that last load in or I would possibly forfeit my $25,000 bond. I looked at the clock by the ER desk. It said 1:00 p.m.! Removing the oxygen mask, I quickly dressed and put on my work boots. I disconnected myself from the monitor last so as not to alert the ER staff that I was leaving.

As soon as I pulled out the monitor cables, I darted out of the room. Lory and Trevor were in the waiting room. When Lory saw me coming he looked surprised. "Bro, you're okay? Let's get you home!"

"No, Lory, we need to get those last few big fir down to the landing for Wade if I'm going to make my fifteen loads in time."

He protested vehemently. I assured him I would be okay. Besides, I couldn't afford to lose twenty-five grand!

We jumped into the truck. Lory drove us back out, still telling me that nothing was worth the risk, especially not my life. I told him I appreciated his concern, but we were getting that last load in on time—no arguments.

We arrived around 1:45. I fired up the Cat and headed back up to those last three logs. Trevor and Lory hooked them up, I winched them tight into the fairlead and down we went. Arriving at the truck, I phoned Wade to come and get the load. Luckily, I was able to get him on his cell. Wade delivered the logs to Safe Enterprise Log Sort at 4:20 p.m. Contract fulfilled!

We took the next couple of days off. It was the first time for me that doing absolutely nothing felt so good. I suffered with a sore chest and overall body pain, having been struck and partly crushed by a nearly two-ton tree, but in a few days it was business as usual—we were back up that sheer mountainside, falling and skidding down more big berries (large, high-value standing timber).

Missed by an Inch

I have had some very close calls over the years, working in so many different fields and locales. Sometimes they happened because of my carelessness and sometimes because of others'. When I was working up at Gilford Island on the west coast of British Columbia, I worked as a dozer operator, welder and swamper on the drill. Blasting quarries for road building can be a dangerous business—in fact, whenever you're dealing with dynamite and heavy equipment, there are always inherent risks.

We had just moved the track drill up to a new area where we had punched in a short road spur to drill a quarry. This quarry would provide the gravel required to finish the sub grade for the logging road.

Our plan was to set up at the north end of the face, where we would drill ten-metre holes horizontally, spaced a metre apart. Once we had about a third of the face drilled off, I would preload the holes with five-centimetre Powerfrac dynamite, putting in twelve to fifteen sticks per hole and leaving a collar of roughly two metres to hold the shot in place. That way the blast would not fly all over the countryside. In addition, the collar would aid in creating more fine gravel and smaller chunks of rock, useful for building a good road that could be graded to keep it in better repair over time and usage.

My driller, Will, was a crusty old man who was not neces-
sarily the best driller I have ever worked with, but he was getting the job done. On our second day of drilling, as per our
plan we had a little more than one-third of the face drilled. I
loaded the holes that were ready for dynamite. I tied in the
first stick with a trunk line and pushed the remaining sticks in
behind, leaving enough line outside of the hole to connect it
to every other hole and using delays, intermittently, to create a
better blast configuration.

I kept on in this fashion as we continued to drill, going along
nicely. I would change drill steels for a while, and when we had
a row of holes drilled, I would preload them while Will started
on the next row of holes one metre over from the last row.

The face was four rows high, nearly two and half metres
high. Standing on a pail, I could reach just high enough to
push each series of dynamite sticks down the holes. I used a
plastic push rod the same length as each drill steel, just over
three metres. Each rod was threaded on either end, one end
male, one female. I joined them together until they were the
required length to cover the distance we needed to drill.

When we were over two-thirds loaded, we had to make a
slight inward turn on the face to where we had been previously
drilling. I used the plastic push rods to line up the drill for the
next series of holes so we'd be parallel to the last hole, ensuring
the same one-metre spacing all the way along.

I placed the push rod into the bottom hole, stood back far
enough to see the angle, then motioned for Will to position
the drill unit at the same angle as the push rod. When I was
satisfied, I gave him the go-ahead signal. While he drilled I
continued to load, starting from the bottom and working my

way up. What we were doing was completely against safety regulations; nevertheless, I kept on loading the holes already drilled and tying in each run that we had loaded. I finished loading and tying in the whole face. It was primed and ready to go just as Will was ready to add the last drill steel to finish the ten metres required.

I changed the steel and watched him push the drill steel back into the hole. Thinking it looked like it was on more of an angle than we had started on, I waved to Will, who kept drilling but acknowledged me by waving his hand questioningly. I gestured with my arms that it looked like the steel was going in crooked and at the wrong angle, that it might drill into the other hole.

He waved his arm sarcastically as if to say, "You're crazy; it's fine!"

He continued to drill. I continued to be concerned. Still not confident in Will's judgment, I walked over close to the drill, which was now almost fully drilled in. I looked down the drill boom, then at my push rod partway into the hole right beside it. I could see by the angle we were drilling that we were within only a few centimetres away from hitting a live hole!

I turned and screamed at Will to stop. He waved me off. I ran to the drill, jumped up and stood right in front of his window, yelling again, "Stop the f—ing drill!" He stopped and jumped out, asking in an angry voice, "Why the hell did you stop me?"

I said nothing. Instead, with 280 sticks of dynamite already loaded and tied into the face, I positioned him where I was standing just a moment before. He looked for a moment, then almost sheepishly replied, "That was very close."

We pulled the steel out of the hole. We placed the other pieces of the push rod into the hole we'd just drilled, and with horror realized we had indeed been, in our estimation, within fifteen centimetres of hitting the loaded hole that was tied in. And if we'd hit it? Well, you can guess the outcome.

We both sat down for a few minutes to ponder what had happened and, more importantly, what could have happened if we had hit that live hole. They say that life can change in a moment, and truly, that was all we'd had left!

Officer Needs Backup

Once or twice a hunting season something happens that is kind of out of the norm, or at least unexpected. That's probably one reason I enjoy it so much. You just never know what is going to happen.

My son Brent and I had decided to head to an area we call Iron River, up where the Oyster River begins its journey heading to meet the sea southwest of Campbell River. I'm not sure if I ever found an Iron River there, but nevertheless, that's what we called it. Brent, now twelve years old, had become an accomplished hunter, and I preferred hunting with him over anyone else.

I loved hunting in those mountains and the valleys that drained the runoff into the Oyster River, which eventually, when all the tributaries joined it on its course, would spill its cold, clear waters into the Pacific Ocean at Oyster Bay. I had taken some nice blacktail bucks and large black bears over the years up there.

It was still early in the season, the middle of September. The days were balmy, sometimes reaching temperatures in the twenty-Celsius range. By mid-morning, everything that had been out and about earlier would now be holed up in the shade of the dark, cool rainforests of Vancouver Island. Nothing was likely to move out into the logging slashes until closer to evening, usually within an hour of last light. As the sun began to rise high into the morning sky, we decided to call it a day and head home.

We saw a few grouse heading down and took a couple to put in the pot for dinner that night. Pan-fried blue grouse are exquisite. We continued on the Comox Logging Road, nearing the Campbell River Airport, southwest of Campbell River and only a few kilometres from town.

Rounding a corner, Brent and I were surprised to see a marked police cruiser parked off to the right of the road. No lights were on and we couldn't see anyone in the vehicle or on the road. We pulled up behind the cruiser, listened for a moment and heard no sounds of life or activity of any sort. Curiosity got the best of me and, wondering if maybe something criminal might have taken place and the officer was down, we climbed out of the truck.

I hollered, "Everything okay?" then waited for a response. There was none. Brent gave me a puzzled look and shrugged his shoulders. I hollered again, "Anyone here?" Then a whisper came: "I'm okay." I asked if there was anything we could do. The voice said, "No, that's all right." Again I inquired, "You sure?" Probably realizing that I would continue to pry, he answered with a little uncertainty, "I just shot a buck."

I looked at Brent and quietly mouthed, "What?" Without being invited we headed into the bush on the opposite side of where we were parked. When we had gone about fifteen metres or so we found a young police officer standing over a nice two-point buck. He looked confused and somewhat embarrassed as we approached him.

Seeing the buck lying there untouched and no knife in

the officer's hand, I could tell the man was out of his element. He looked like a child who just been caught with his hand in the cookie jar. I asked how it was going and he apologetically replied, "I've never shot a deer before, and I don't know what to do next."

Well, it was obvious that wasn't his only problem. First: he'd used his service revolver to shoot the deer so he would have to explain to his superiors why he had fired his revolver. Second: he was in full uniform, and it would be kind of hard to explain all the blood on his clothes after he dressed his buck. Third: he was on duty! Fourth: how would he get it home?

Now, I could have been a real nasty guy but I guess I still have the odd soft spot for people in trouble, and this young cop was in trouble. Looking at my son, I asked, "Do you want to dress this deer for him?" Brent agreed, and a very relieved cop gratefully accepted the help.

Once Brent finished, I asked the officer if he wanted me to take his buck anywhere specific. "No, that's okay. You've done plenty already," he said, adding that he had contacted his wife and she was coming with their pickup to get the deer. He asked whether we wouldn't mind telling her exactly where he was if we chanced to see her on our way home. She would be driving a white Chev half-ton pickup and had blond hair.

"Sure, no problem," I assured him. Brent and I hopped in the truck, the cop still keeping a low profile in the bush, then headed on our way.

Soon we came to the Elk River Timber (ERT) junction with the Comox Logging Road and turned right toward town. We had gone a couple hundred metres when a white Chev pickup came into view around a corner. As it slowly approached us I could see the driver, a blond woman in her twenties, looking lost and searching from side to side of the gravel road.

I slowed to a halt and put my hand out to stop her. When she did, I explained to a very scared and confused lady where her husband was and gave her directions to his squad car. She thanked me profusely and headed on her way.

Brent remarked, "We could have got that cop in so much trouble if we wanted to!" I agreed but said sometimes people just needed a break.

Six weeks later, coming from hockey at the arena near the Rockland subdivision, I was in a bit of a hurry and was driving somewhat over the speed limit. Suddenly a cop was hot on my tail, lights flashing for me to pull over to the side of the road. I did so on Evergreen Road, then waited for the fine that I was certain to receive. I knew I wouldn't be able to talk my way out of it as I'd been doing thirty kilometres over the speed limit!

I grabbed my insurance from the glove compartment and handed it and my licence to the officer, who was now standing by my door. All I could see was his torso. I didn't want to give him respect or acknowledge that he was even there, so I held out my paperwork without looking.

After he looked at my driver's licence he bent down so he was at eye level with me. I turned to look and saw this cop with a big smile on his face. "I thought it was you," he said pleasantly. "How're you doing?"

Imagine my surprise to recognize the police officer Brent and I had met out in the bush! My demeanour changed as I happily responded, "Doing good, how about you?"

"Same here." I asked if he had been out hunting lately. A little red-faced, he responded, "Not since I met you and your son."

He smiled, handed back my papers, patted my shoulder, told me to have a great day and proceeded back to his cruiser. I pulled out and waved my hand out the window. He blinked his lights then did a U-turn and drove away.

Like I'd told Brent six weeks earlier, "Sometimes people just need a break." And I'd just got mine!

Lights Out

Boxing has been a big part of my life, with my involvement as both a boxer and a coach encompassing almost four decades. I have seen my sons Kelly Bruce Jr., Wade, Isaac, and Jacob, and my daughter Samantha, along with many other fine amateur and professional boxers, obtain numerous accolades and championships over those years. And I've witnessed—and been a part of—many memorable fights.

I started boxing competitively in 1984 at twenty-nine years of age, which is late in life for a boxer. I had no aspirations, but I caught the bug soon after my son joined the Campbell River Eagles Boxing Club. While I was waiting for Kelly to finish a workout, head coach George Shiels came over and said if I was going to be there anyway, I might as well join the club and train, so I did. After a couple of workouts, George asked if I had ever fought before—I told him I had, but never in a boxing ring. He said I had pretty good technique and lots of power, and encouraged me to take a match. So I did. My first opponent was a young buck from Victoria named Scott. The fight was stopped in the second round—I landed some solid straight rights and I think I broke two of his ribs. I was hooked!

George Shiels was a good man with a cranky disposition— at least, that was how I saw him. He had a short fuse and was not very patient. It was definitely his way or the highway. After I'd been training with him for a while, he approached me one day and informed me that I was scheduled to fight a boxer named Ron. The fight was less than one month away, in our hometown of Campbell River.

That was almost all he said about the fight—or, in fact, about my opponent. But he did mention that I would be fighting as a light heavyweight. I was surprised and confused—I was a heavyweight and my first three bouts up to that date had been fought as a heavyweight. I weighed ninety kilos with 14 per cent body fat, and dropping to light heavy was going to be a challenge and extremely taxing on my body. Dropping to eighty-one kilos, the light heavy maximum weight, in one month was going to take near starvation.

At the time, I worked as an underground millwright in the Westmin Resources mine at Myra Falls. It was both a physically and intellectually demanding job. One day, just over a week into my diet of carrot sticks and a lettuce and tomato sandwich for my lunch mainstay, I passed out underground. A moment or two later I recovered and was taken above ground to first aid, where I spent the rest of the afternoon until quitting time.

Even after that, I continued to starve myself until, finally, fight day came. At 11:00 a.m., I headed to the weigh-in and medical checkup, which was held at the Campbell River Community Hall. The fight would be later in the evening.

As I walked into the hall, I noticed a guy around my size and safely assumed it was my opponent. As was customary in my previous fights, I went to greet Ron and wish him the best—first, because I believe I am a good sport, and second, if he had a good fight and I beat him, I would be beating him at his best!

I reached Ron and extended my hand in greeting. He looked at me with a wry smirk, slapped my hand away and laughed at me. Caught off guard, I turned away and for probably the first time ever felt a bit intimidated by another fighter, whether in the street or the ring. The day dragged, and the encounter at the weigh-in dogged me and troubled me the entire time.

Finally, it was almost showtime. The hall was filled with anticipation of the upcoming event. I was undefeated in my short three-fight career, and Ron, I had found out earlier in the day, was undefeated too. He was also an open fighter. That meant he had been in at least ten fights (although I believe that number was considerably higher). In the fight game, that could be considered as lopsided as Mike Tyson fighting Pee-wee Herman.

While I was in the dressing room, a former boxer from the same Eagles boxing club, John Hunter, approached as I was waiting to be gloved up. With plenty of emotion, he implored me to "Knock the f—er out!"

Minutes later I was led out by my head coach, George, and my assistant coach, Charles (Charlie) John. We entered the ring, and the building was full of both spectators and energy. Bert Lowes was an experienced referee, and he also was famous for being knocked out while reffing a bout between Canadian champion Willie DeWit and Cuban fighter Pedro Cardenas.

Bert called Ron and me to the centre of the ring for last-minute instructions and to ask for a clean fight, then sent us to our respective corners to await the first round. The bell rang and we approached each other cautiously—but only for a moment. Then Ron dealt me a barrage of head-snapping jabs with an equally impressive onslaught of hooks and stiff right hands. I felt as if I was surrounded. He was quicker and far more skilled than me, without question.

I struggled to stay on my feet. I was being humiliated and beaten up in my hometown arena, and there was nothing I could do to stop it. I may have landed a couple of jabs, but that was the extent of my offence. Nearing the end of the first round (and I must say it could not have come quick enough), I saw George stride away from my corner in disgust with his hands in the air. Fully demoralized, what little hope I might have had left was now completely gone.

Mercifully the bell rang to end the first round and I staggered groggily back to my stool. George, returning to the corner, yelled in my face, "You look like a bum! What the hell you doing out there? Knock this guy out!" I pleaded to be told how I could do that, as so far, I could not get a glove on him.

Charlie rubbed my shoulder encouragingly and in his unique Jamaican way said, "Man, you just fight your fight, don't give up, you can beat this guy!"

The ten-second warning buzzer sounded. Charlie gave me a pat on the back and even George said, "You can do this!"

The second round started much like the first. It was an onslaught. I got a few shots in but nothing with any power, as he was able to deflect or move his head quick enough to lessen the impact. Midway through the round, Ron got a little hungrier for a knockout. He obviously was not aware that that was going to be a very difficult task. I had only been knocked out once in my life, by my tough oldest brother Robin, who did it when I was twelve years old.

He now tried to load up his punches, getting just a little wider and leaving a little more time and space for me to counter. At one point he had me pinned against the ropes, and after a short barrage he opened up to throw what he hoped would be the knockout left hook. He never got to land it. I recoiled off the ropes, finally getting the opening I needed, and landed one of my best straight right hands. His eyes rolled back in his head and he fell forward toward me. As he slumped, I threw one of the most vicious uppercuts I had ever thrown, in pure anger and frustration.

Ron's head snapped back ninety degrees to his shoulders, and he hit the ring floor with a resounding thud. Moving fast, the fight doctor jumped into the ring as he began to convulse wildly, his legs shaking and jerking in fitful spasms. A few minutes later they had him on his stool, still under intense observation.

I was more angry than elated. I was glad to see my opponent flat on his back and out cold, especially after the way he'd treated me at the weigh-in and the stress it caused me all day. However, I was angry because I might have ultimately won the war, but I'd lost the battle—at least all but four seconds of the fight.

John Hunter came into the dressing room while I was getting my hand wraps off, absolutely elated, to congratulate me. I later found out why George Shiels was so intent on me fighting Young and why John was so happy I'd won. Ron had apparently knocked out John and another fighter of George's. They wanted payback, and indeed they got it—at my expense.

I was told later that Ron quit boxing under doctor's orders, and as I continued my boxing career, I never saw him again.

A couple years later, and much like before, George approached me and told me he had a guy he wanted me to fight in an upcoming club show a little over a month away. He did not say who, nor did I ask or care, having competed in quite a few more bouts at a pretty high level. After knocking out Ron, who was an open-class fighter, I automatically became open class myself—or, as they call it now in amateur boxing, an elite fighter. I continued training.

Meanwhile, the opponent, also unaware of who he was fighting, was training as well. It was none other than Ron. Tony Duffy, a member of the British Columbia boxing team who had fought with me as a team member in the 1988 Olympic trials for Seoul, Korea, had apparently been apprised of who Ron would be fighting. This was only hearsay, as I obviously was not privy to their conversation, but he asked Young if he was ready to fight again, in what would be his first comeback fight. Ron told him he was good to go. Tony then asked if he knew who he would fighting. Ron said it didn't matter, to which Tony replied, "It might. You're fighting Ricketts again." To which Ron apparently replied, "F— that. I am not ever fighting him again!"

We never did fight again. In fact, I fought another tough heavyweight instead, John Flewin, and won a unanimous decision. Flewin and I would fight again a couple years later, post-Olympics, in Vancouver. That night we fought like lions, throwing caution to the wind, much to the praise of the packed Agrodome. I lost the decision to the judges, but Flewin's former coach, Boyd Baynes, came to me after and told me it could have gone either way and he thought I'd won. Seeing as I had fought that night with a broken hand from an accident six weeks earlier, I was okay with the outcome!

Okanagan Idol 1965

Christmas morning 1964 was a very important day in my life and will always stand as a watershed moment in my development. It would have a major impact on my ability to deal with the difficult times I would face in my life, not only back then but to this very day. What could have been so significant to me as an nine-year-old child? My first guitar!

My dad had come to our place for Christmas—shortly after our move to Kelowna. After that move, he would seldom be part of our lives, although as a young man I would end up working with him in Vernon and on Vancouver Island. I love my dad and did then too; that never changed no matter what happened. (Now he's nearly ninety-five years old and still living on his own somewhere out in the bush on Vancouver Island!) Anyway, Dad would come for his yearly "quell my guilt" trip—to play the hero and give us children a couple of bucks' worth of goods—then he would be on his way until he was feeling guilty again.

I am not entirely sure why that particular year he bought me a guitar, but I was excited to receive it nonetheless. He handed me the large cardboard case it was wrapped in along with a book called *Alfred's Teach Yourself to Play Guitar*, and after I opened the box he simply said, "Go learn how to play it." Straight to the basement I went. One hour later I returned to the living room, where some of my siblings were still play-ing with a few toys they had received. My mother and father were sitting on the couch watching my brothers and sisters play.

My dad asked if I had got it all figured out yet. I replied in my stuttering voice that I—I—I—had. I sat on a kitchen chair and began to play an old classic song that I'd heard my mom and dad play when I was a very small child, "Mama Don't Allow." I strummed and sang as best I could. The song actually did resemble the version I'd heard. When I was finished, there were nods of approval.

That was my start of learning how to cope with a bad stut-tering problem. I found that when I played and sang, I could speak flawlessly and without any fear or trepidation about what might actually come out.

I played as often as I was allowed to at home until I met a new friend, Rod Sterling, early in 1965, and he and I began to practise together. He played the tambourine and a single snare drum. Most of the time we practised at his parents' place. We even attempted to learn some of the Beatles' hits. They were the most famous band anywhere, and everyone wanted to be the Beatles!

Rod was absolutely fearless about playing in front of any-one even though he, too, was only nine years old. I was not as confident when it came to playing in front of anyone other than his or my family. So I was shocked and horrified when he told me he had asked our principal if we could play a couple of songs at the Thanksgiving assembly, which was to be held in our school gym. Rod wanted to learn two new Beatles songs, and Thanksgiving was only two weeks away!

The principal agreed heartily and said it would be a wonderful idea. Rod found me at first recess to tell me the good news. "What!" was my reaction. "Are you crazy? We can't play in front of the whole school!" Oozing with confidence, Rod patted my arm and replied, "We're great! They'll love us!" I don't know why I did but I actually believed him, at least enough to agree to play.

The morning came for the school assembly. Rod and I tried to keep it a secret but most of the kids in our grade knew. However, the rest of the elementary school, for the most part, thought it was just another school assembly. The principal would wish us a happy Thanksgiving and tell us to be safe and have fun.

Our teacher, Miss Gerlinger, set up the record player just offstage with the Beatles' 45-rpm record for us to play and sing along with. Rod was playing his tambourine and I, my guitar. We stood offstage while the principal gave his address. When he was finished, he motioned Rod and me onstage and told those in attendance that they were in for a special treat: two of their fellow students, Rod Sterling and Kelly Ricketts, were now going to entertain them with a couple of songs.

A chair was moved near a microphone for me to sit with my guitar, while Rod would stand by my side and play his tambourine. I nervously looked out at the huge crowd. Okay, it may have been only 150 people, but to an eight-year-old it might as well have been the world. We looked over at Miss Gerlinger for our cue, and she dropped the needle on the vinyl and gave us the thumbs-up.

"A Hard Day's Night" began—I fumbled for a moment then found my place and began to play. Once I started, I became almost oblivious to those out front. I just dropped my head, played and sang as if it was just me in the room. The song finished, people clapped and even a little cheering could be heard. Miss Gerlinger flipped over the 45 and placed the needle down for "She Loves You."

With much more enthusiasm we played as hard and as loud as we could, and I even looked up at the people watching us intently from the gym floor. I was a mix of emotions: I felt terrified and also justified—that I finally kind of belonged in this world and had something to offer. The song soon ended and again applause and even more cheering rewarded Rod's and my effort.

We bowed our heads and ran offstage, conquerors of the world. My sister Penny, who was in Grade 2, was watching with a friend who exclaimed, "Boy, is your brother ever good!" In hindsight, I think if Rod and I had just stood there with our mouths hanging open and the Beatles record playing by itself, we would have had a similar response—it was the Beatles they were cheering for!

That experience opened a door for me that would allow me to communicate my deepest feelings, ones that I would never have been able to express in any other way. Music was a huge confidence booster for me, and it became my most influential medium for sharing how I really felt. Where I once could not effectively communicate my feelings, I could now disguise them in music—after all, almost everyone understands music.

That Christmas gift was one of the best gifts I have ever received and it brought me through many storms in my life. It has borne me up when I felt sometimes that I was completely alone. Thank you to both my fathers for this gift—my earthly father, Bruce, and my Heavenly Father. Oh yes, and to Rod Sterling, for talking me into playing at that assembly in the first place!

Jump or Die

It is hard to find a more beautiful place anywhere in the world than the west coast of British Columbia: majestic coastal mountains, and endless bays to offer protection and a place to drop anchor and set out the crab traps. You will see porpoises racing along in your bow wake, killer and grey whales spending their summers on a lazy migration to distant destinations, as well as orcas that are full-time residents of the waters from Haida Gwaii to Victoria to the west side of Vancouver Island and its inside passage, the Salish Sea.

I have spent many decades flying to remote logging camps all along this coast and, on a clear day, the view is simply amazing. However, travelling by boat is by far the most rewarding. Every inlet, fjord and bay has some historical legacy. Remnants can be found of the habitations of the coast's earlier peoples and the different businesses they operated there, such as at Namu, a former major canning and fish-processing village. It is nestled into the hillside just south of the opening of Burke Channel on the inside passage.

With my second wife Ingrid, who blessed my life by marrying me and adding six more sweet children to my world, I purchased thirty-two hectares of gorgeous coastal property just east of the northernmost tip of Vancouver Island in Smith Inlet, more precisely Millbrook Cove. My hope was to build a resort to service the ever-growing ecotourism industry, especially whale-watching and grizzly-viewing excursions, as there were plenty of both in the area, and to provide access to the world-class salmon fishing. The property consisted of nearly two kilometres of waterfront with three separate small bays that were connected to a larger bay, Millbrook Cove. They were protected from the strong westerly winds that would often blow in from distant reaches in the vast Pacific Ocean.

The cove created such good protection that many fishing boats and yachts would anchor in our bay to wait out the winds. These westerly winds could come quickly, with little warning. If you were not privy to a current marine weather forecast or were simply not paying attention, you could find yourself in some significantly turbulent seas.

I had purchased a thirty-two-foot live-aboard Tollycraft with a diesel motor. This boat was not made for speed but more for comfort, and with twin large fuel tanks, it had a range of about 950 kilometres. I thought one day I might decide to travel to Alaska, and the long range was a factor in my purchase of the boat.

I launched the boat out of Brown's Bay in Campbell River one day in early May, hoping to make Millbrook Cove by nightfall to set up camp for the selective logging I had planned. I was accompanied by a young friend, Christopher, the son of my dear friends Wolf and Trish Sellmer. Wolf wanted me to give him an experience that city life would never afford him. The trip was one problem after another, though. We had continual problems with our out-drive shaft. It was a V drive and the CV axle kept breaking. We finally ended up in Millbrook

Cove after doing needed repairs in Port Hardy, situated near the north end of Vancouver Island. My sons Kelly Jr. and Wade joined us there to continue on to the property and to help with getting a beachhead established. My machines and welding truck and our trailer (for accommodation) were being brought by barge.

We sailed into the cove early in the afternoon. Finding two dolphins (pilings) in the centre bay where it would be protected, we secured the boat there. The pilings would keep it in enough water when the tide went out. We also wanted to secure it by tying a beach line to a gnarly spruce that hung out over the rocks of the beach below.

It wasn't a complicated plan, but our troubles were far from over, it seemed. Heading for the tree, I clambered over the rocks below it with my caulk boots on. These boots were great for walking on wet logs, giving good traction with small spikes that layered the bottom of the soles, but unfortunately they were not so good on hard coastal granite. As I reached out as far and as high up the windswept spruce as I could, my foot slipped on the rocks, catapulting me forward. I went three metres straight down, headfirst, throwing my hands in front of my face to protect it from the sharp, barnacle-encrusted boulders.

My right arm struck full force, saving my face and head from serious injury; however, my forearm was torn open from elbow to wrist. The wound looked quite hideous; I could see tendons and nerves twitching, though it only bled for a moment. You could imagine what those barnacles might have done to my face—no scalpel-like precision, just a ragged fraying of flesh to the bone.

Kelly Jr. implored me to use our satellite phone to call in a seaplane from Port Hardy, which could get me to the hospital before infection could set in. It seemed Kelly had had to insist on me doing something for my welfare once or twice before. I calmly told him that the best disinfectant I knew of was only a short distance away. I walked out into half a metre of water and swished my exposed wound in the salty brine. I continued to rinse out the wound and pick out the last few pieces of broken barnacles and dirt wedged into the cut.

Opening my first-aid pack, I pulled out some tensor bandages and two maxi-flow feminine pads (yes, I carried feminine hygiene products with me—they are perfect for protecting wounds of any type). I covered the wound with the two maxi-pads, then, squeezing the gaping wound together, I had Kelly wrap the tensor bandages tightly around my arm.

We did little during the next few days. On the third day I removed my bandages and was shocked to see that my forearm was already knit back together. It wasn't pretty but there was no redness or ooze that might signify infection. In fact, I felt so confident I began falling trees for the camp the very next day.

* * *

I would make a few more trips in and out of the cove over the next year. Once we had established a beachhead, the Tollycraft would stayed moored for most of the summer, and my seventeen-foot aluminum crew boat would be primarily used for trips to get fuel and food supplies. And to go to Port Hardy, where my vehicle was parked at the Port Hardy airport. My Tollycraft would stay moored to the pilings, safe until I returned the following August with my friend Ron. I had promised Ron some stellar fishing for salmon and halibut and, being an avid fisherman himself, he jumped at the opportunity.

We left Port Hardy at mid-morning in my crew boat and arrived at Millbrook Cove around 1:00 p.m. Camp had been set up for the past three months. The thirty-five-foot Dutchmen travel trailer was our home base, with three bunks and a large bedroom. I built a small porch to hold wet work clothes and some of our outdoor gear and added a five-thousand-watt generator as our power source. We stowed our duffle bags of gear in our rooms and fired up the generator to plug in my sixteen-cubic-foot freezer. It was empty, but we hoped to fill it shortly with delicious West Coast salmon, sea bass and halibut. The bonus was the nice low tides we could take advantage of to fill our quota of large and tasty Dungeness crab.

The north end of the bay was absolutely chock full of these big, beautiful crustaceans. Along with the low tide, all that was needed was a fishing net. We drifted slowly across the eel grass and when we spotted a legal crab we just scooped it up. It took less than fifteen minutes to reach both our limits of crab. It was incredible.

According to a Coast Guard fellow I talked to shortly after purchasing the property, my thirty-two hectares of waterfront was the most beautiful place on the whole west coast of British Columbia. He said that included all the way to the Aleutians in Alaska, and added that the best crabbing was right in my bay. He was absolutely correct on the crabbing, and as for the most beautiful place, I might argue that a bit, but he wasn't far off.

After cleaning our catch of delicious Dungeness crab, Ron and I headed off for what promised to be equally productive fishing. I had found a particularly good spot a few weeks ear-lier that was going to deliver the goods. Ten minutes later we had lines in the water. "Fish on!" were the most oft-repeated words heard as we hooked fat sea bass and greenling cod within seconds of dropping our lines in the water. I knew there were salmon there but we couldn't get down far enough with our lines because they were immediately hit by the frenetic sea bass. It was certainly nothing to be upset about as the bass were delicious.

That said, I had promised Ron some big springs and nice coho. Realizing we had to find a way to get our lines under the bass, a plan came to mind. We would simply move out from the glory hole, drop our lines down to the twenty-four-metre depth where the salmon would be, then slowly motor back into our hot spot. It worked perfectly. We drifted in just under the sea bass and "Fish on!" was heard again, only this time it was salmon. We double headed on two nice springs; mine was around six kilos and Ron's about eleven. We had a day and a half before Ron had to be back in Kamloops, so we caught two fine coho then headed back to camp. We got back around 4:00 p.m. with sixteen sea bass, two greenling cod and twenty-five kilograms of salmon. It was a good day!

The next day the westerlies started to pick up again, so we waited in camp and went crabbing in the inside cove. Around lunchtime a fifty-six-foot yacht pulled in and anchored out in the bay, waiting, we figured, for the wind to subside. As we were returning from another crab catch, we saw a couple standing on the deck at the stern. They waved a friendly hello so we idled over and introduced ourselves. They were Carol and Bob Stevens, a couple in their early fifties out of Port

Angeles in Washington state. After visiting for a short while, we bid farewell and took in our catch of crab to clean. We had nearly one good-sized cooler full of succulent Dungeness crab.

After a dinner of fresh crab in garlic butter, we headed back out for the evening bite, and again our limit of sea bass and salmon was the result. We arrived back with about two hours of daylight left so we decided to get another limit of crabs, then visit with the Stevenses and two of their friends who had joined them on their trip. We took them a few crabs for their dinner, which they graciously accepted. Even though they had some crab pots out, these only caught small, illegal crabs that had to be released. I had found through experience that the large, legal crabs refused to go into the traps set out for them.

After we climbed aboard their yacht, Bob asked who owned the nice Tollycraft. I told him the *K&B* was mine, but the out-drive was in need of repair and I would have it towed to Port Hardy where I could get special tools and any parts I might need to work on it. Bob gladly offered to tow my boat in for me tomorrow morning, but very early, as the marine forecast was for calm seas of one metre until they would increase with stronger winds. A bigger swell was expected by around 9:30 a.m.

We thought we could be on our way by shortly after daybreak, which would give us a bit more than three hours before the winds would increase. The Stevenses were heading back that way regardless, so they assured us they would be more than happy to tow it. We agreed—Ron and I had plenty of crab, sea bass and salmon, and Ron had to leave sometime the next day anyway so we passed on the morning fishing.

Before daylight, Ron and I had the seventeen-foot crew boat loaded with our bounty from the sea and our gear. We untied the *K&B* and towed it over to the Stevenses' yacht. We had thirty metres of three-centimetre heavy-duty tow line, which we hooked to a towing cleat on the stern of the yacht and the bow of the *K&B*. We double-checked everything before we were off according to plan.

The water was dead calm as we pulled out of Millbrook Cove and into Smith Inlet. Our speed would not be too impressive, but even at eleven knots we would be in behind Vancouver Island and out of the open sea by the time the wind began to build. Well, that's what we hoped.

As we motored along behind Table Island and the Egg Island lighthouse, it was beginning to get a touch choppy, but the yacht, the *K&B* and Ron and I following in the crew boat were travelling along just fine.

At the southernmost part of Egg Island, the sea was now becoming angry—a full two hours ahead of schedule. The rollers were already coming in at two and a half metres and building steadily as we passed the nearly submerged Iron Rock about a hundred metres south of the coastline.

We continued on, keeping a watchful eye out and wishing we could travel about ten knots faster. The *K&B* began to rise and drop much more significantly. Sometimes the Stevenses' ship would go down into the trough on one side while the *K&B* went up the other, putting great strain on the tow rope. Undaunted, we continued. But within minutes, the wind doubled in force, blowing just a few knots under gale force, and a rough chop was created at the top of each big wave.

Then a sight I would not soon forget gripped me in fear. Less than half a kilometre away, I could see a huge wave bearing down from where it originated deep in the Pacific. It towered above the nearly three-metre seas we were in already. I hollered to Ron to hold on and stay low. I positioned the bow of the little open crew boat to meet the wave head-on. In all its malevolence it hit us like a tank. We shot up into the air, then dropped deep into the trough of the next big sweeper. After that they came relentlessly, one after another, each successive wave becoming stronger and higher.

Searching for the Stevenses' boat, I caught sight of the *K&B* just in time to see the tow rope snap off the bow of my boat. We tried going back to the Tolly to reconnect the tow, but the sea was having none of that. I watched forlornly as the pounding sea pushed my beautiful boat farther away toward an impending meeting with the rocky west coast beach.

Turning my attention back to the Stevenses' boat, I could see them about a hundred metres away. Carol Stevens was standing at the stern, waving frantically for us to catch up to them and jump to safety on their ship. Needless to say, this would prove to be far easier said than done. We caught up to the Stevenses' boat. At times it was so low in the trough of the giant wave ahead of us that its radar device and ship flag, which were eleven metres from the water line, would completely disappear.

We were able to manoeuvre into position behind their stern. As it rode up on each large wave, I could see the underside of their yacht. It would sit suspended for a brief moment before again dropping into another deep trough. We were not going to get many chances before we would have no more to take. We needed to get on the bigger boat, now!

With Carol and their male friend waving frantically at us, I told Ron he would have to climb onto the bow of the boat. I would get us as close as I could and when I yelled to jump, he needed to go *right then!* Ron looked at me with terror in his eyes—this was something he had never prepared for and I, with all my years on the ocean, was not much better prepared.

Making another attempt, we had to time Ron's jump precisely for the moment when both boats simultaneously met at the top of a wave. Then, as the Stevenses' yacht began to drop into the bottom of the wave, and when we were nearly level with their deck at the stern, Ron would jump. It started to work as planned: Ron managed to crawl out onto the bow. Both boats were in position. I yelled, "Now, Ron! Jump!" But Ron was frozen in fear, and the brief moment we had was lost.

I hollered again at Ron as he held on to the bow rails with a death grip, the sea becoming angrier and more intense. "You need to jump, Ron, or we're both going to lose our lives!" I again positioned our small boat near the stern, and at the exact moment throttled the 90-horse Mercruiser into place. Realizing I was a little too close and fearing that we would end up underneath the heaving stern of the bigger boat, I slammed the control into reverse. There was a funny clunk, and the boat would not respond, instead coming dangerously near to being crushed by the yacht.

This was going to make it a nearly impossible task. If we were going to pull this evacuation off, it would now take a miracle of timing and divine intervention. I heard myself yelling at my dear friend Ron with more force and intensity. Gingerly, I moved the boat into position. Finally, a minute or so later, we were ready to attempt another rescue.

As loud as I could scream above the intense winds and the crashing sea, I hollered to Ron, "You need to jump off this damn boat *NOW!*" As if that finally woke Ron up, he jumped for all he was worth. Both Carol and their friend grabbed Ron's arms as he landed tenuously on their swim grid. With Ron aboard, I felt some relief. At least I would not be responsible for his death.

I now had to do the same thing for myself as I'd done for Ron: position the boat at the exact time and place it needed to be, take the bow rope, jump over the windshield run to the end of the bow, then jump to safety. This all had to take place in less than three seconds or I would be jumping to my death and burial in the cold, unforgiving sea.

Time and again I tried to get into position. However, with no reverse, the task became substantially more difficult. I would still need to complete every other detail in less time than most would say their phone number. Each time felt like my last chance, as both the Stevenses' fifty-six-foot yacht and my seventeen-foot crew boat were now getting buffeted cross-ways and the boats began to yaw port to starboard.

Then the moment came. I was in position. Putting the boat in neutral, I dove over the windshield. As I came to my feet the yacht was dropping down another wave. I took two quick steps and jumped with all the spring my shaking legs could muster. I caught a railing with my right hand and the Stevenses' friend and Ron grabbed for my left hand and my bow line, which was clutched tightly in it. As we were getting back inside the yacht, Bob navigated the ship as quickly and safely as he could back in the direction we had come from—if we were to continue on, we would still have eleven to thirteen kilometres of open sea to navigate. If we could turn the ship around, we would have only one and a half kilometres to be back in behind Egg and Table Islands and protected from the huge seas.

We had issued a mayday to the Coast Guard, but because of the treacherous seas, they were not even able to respond, at least not anywhere near as quickly as required. Thanks to Bob and Carol's good seafaring skills, though, we were soon back in more protected waters, heading back to Millbrook Cove. But their yacht was a mess. Furniture and plants had been tossed everywhere and even their large refrigerator was flopped over on its side.

As we were nearing Millbrook Cove, the lighthouse keepers at Egg Island radioed out to us—apparently they had witnessed what was happening and how we had lost my thirty-two-foot Tolly. They asked for whoever had lost the boat that was adrift to respond. Carol did, acknowledging that we had lost the tow and hadn't seen it again.

The fellow on the radio replied, "Not to worry. It's drifting up Smith Inlet behind Table Island and it looks fine." Our fear of it crashing onto the reef at Extended Neck never materialized; by some divine intervention, it drifted by the reef safely then began its protected drift up the inlet. It was soon recovered and towed back to the bay where it had sat for the last three months, safe to moor for another month before finally being repaired.

My good buddy Ron tragically lost his life a few years later—far too soon. I hope that he is still able, where he rests to await his glory, to remember our trip fondly, in spite of the terror of that day!

Post-Game Action

A family pastime that seemed to dominate the Ricketts house was fighting. Not sure why exactly, but violence seemed to be ever-present. Don't misunderstand me: in some ways I liked the fact that we learned to fight and take care of ourselves in a tough situation, if it arose. However, I feel that it was more of an everyday experience than was remotely healthy. Nevertheless, that is how it was.

Fortunately, my uncle talked my mother into letting me play ball when I was twelve years old. Up until then I had not been involved in sports of any kind, other than what I'd played at my school, West Rutland Elementary, which was not far from where we lived on Findlay Road.

One Saturday in late May, I was at my ball practice at a ball field not far from our home. I was just finishing up my practice when my brother Terry and a couple of his buddies drove into the park. Terry waved me over to the car. When I ran over and asked what he wanted, he told me to get in the car. I asked why again. He told me to just get in! I ran and got my glove, then hopped into the back seat, curious about why he wanted me to join them. Terry did not hang out with me at all, as a rule.

As we drove out of the park, I asked him one more time: "Why?" Looking straight ahead, he simply said some guys were bad-mouthing me and they needed to be ass-kicked. The Ricketts name had to be defended! I grew worried. I was not a hardened or seasoned fighter like my brothers. You might say I would've rather been a lover and only fought when I had no choice. Now I was going to fight for the sake of nothing, or at least I felt it was nothing.

The Rutland Ball Park was empty except for three guys standing down by the washrooms at the park's west end. We pulled up and parked in front of the bathrooms. I sat looking out at the three guys, all about fifteen years old at least. I knew they were from the high school across the street. I had seen at least two of the guys a couple of times, walking to the corner store just down from both schools. But I had no idea why they would have a beef with me.

I half pleaded with Terry, "I don't want to fight anyone. I don't even know why I would have any reason to fight them." The three guys just stood there waiting, looking almost as confused as I was.

Terry turned to me sitting in the back seat, then related what had happened less than an hour earlier. He explained how he and his buddies were in the Tastee-Freez having a burger when he overheard these three guys talking about how they could beat me up. One of them said, "Yeah, I could kick the shit out of that Ricketts kid," adding that he didn't think the Ricketts brothers were that tough anyway.

They were totally unaware that sitting just a metre away was Terry Ricketts, probably the Ricketts who loved to fight the most. Even though Terry was only a bit older, he decided right there that it was time I learned to take care of the Ricketts name, and myself in particular.

Terry, looking over at the main mouthpiece talking most of the trash, told him, "Yeah, man, I agree. Those Ricketts brothers think they're some big shit. I would love to see someone kick a Ricketts ass!"

The three guys laughed, obviously not knowing who he was. One of the guys replied that first chance he got he was going to lay a beating on Kelly. Terry responded that he knew where I was and was sure he could get me into town, then they could teach me something and he would cover for them if I tried calling the cops. They either were not too bright or figured that they now had no choice, because they agreed.

I got out of the back seat. Still wearing my ball uniform and cleats, I fearfully followed Terry over to where these three were waiting. One had a small length of chain about forty centimetres long, and another was wearing brass knuckles. Seeing this, Terry simply said, "Hey guys, there are three of you against one, so lose the brass knuckles and chain." They tossed them aside. I knew there was no way out of this situation because if I didn't fight them, I would be fighting Terry. And I figured my chances were better with the three strangers.

I took a few steps forward, squared off and we got at it. The guy who had been wielding the chain jumped at me, throwing a wild haymaker. I stepped back and countered with a well-placed kick, catching him under the chin. He fell back, and from then on all I could remember was that I threw a lot of kicks and punches and landed most of them. I know I took a few but I was able to stay on my feet.

Their plan was clear: try to get me off my feet then swarm me. I knew if they did that, I was going to be in a bad way. I used my cleats to keep them off, only throwing punches when they got past my feet.

They lost their desire for fighting after another well-placed kick met the side of the brass-knuckles guy's head. His name was Charlie. He dropped to his knees as blood ran down his temple. The other two pleaded with me to stop.

By this time my fear had turned to anger and rage. I wanted to continue. But Terry ran and grabbed my arm as I was just about to kick the one named Charlie as he kneeled on the ground. "They've had enough!" Terry hissed at me.

I backed up a step while Terry confronted the three previously tough guys and with a large amount of pride declared, "This is what you get when you f— with a Ricketts. This is my brother Kelly. You better remember what happens when you shoot your mouth off. One of us will be closing it for good!" He added, "Do you understand?" They nodded their heads in unison.

We got into the car and Terry and his friends drove me home. Before they took off again, Terry said, "Well done, little brother," and gave me a hug.

The irony of this situation was that the three guys ended up seeking me out to be their friend. Their names were Charlie, Larry and, I think, Dean. I only saw Dean a couple of times but hung out with the other two for about two years until I left home and went to work in Christian Valley, up near Beaverdell. I never saw Larry or Charlie again. Not sure if I learned anything that day, or if they did.

Shallow Dive

Upper Quinsam, or, as some of the old-timers called it, the Argonaut, west of Campbell River about twenty-seven kilometres, was one of my favourite places to hunt bear. Late August offered good opportunities to run into a lot of bears. Plenty of wild berries, such as blueberries and huckleberries, were out, a more than adequate food supply for bears to fatten up for late fall and the winter to follow.

Bob R. and Bob C. (who I'll call Carmen to cut down on confusion) dropped by early one Saturday in 1976 and asked if I wanted to go up to Upper Quinsam to scout for some bears and deer. "Sure," I replied.

I grabbed a couple of soft drinks, made a quick sandwich and we headed out. As the morning turned into early afternoon the bears would be back in the shade, out of the late summer heat, and more than likely stay there until dusk. I didn't think I'd be able to stand being out in the midday heat wearing a thick black fur coat either.

When we got to the area, we cruised around to some of the different lakes and enjoyed just being outdoors. By 3:00 p.m. we were thinking about going for a swim in one of the lakes. It would be a refreshing pastime. We had no shorts so our options were either our birthday suits or underwear—until we put our feet in the water, that is. It was not going to happen, as the lakes had not warmed up much at all from the winter runoff.

We continued on exploring every little road we found, finally coming out to the concrete flume that flowed out of Upper Quinsam to Gooseneck Lake. Stopping beside the gate that controlled the water flow out of the lake, we walked over to stand on the top of the concrete dam where the gate control was mounted; it was locked in a partially open position.

Carmen had been complaining about the heat from sitting in the middle of my single-cab truck without the pleasure of hanging an arm out the open window to get some of the cooling breeze. Pulling off his shirt, he announced he was going to dive off the dam. It was nearly two and half metres high above the running water in the flume.

We cautioned him to check the depth of the water first and he agreed. Climbing back down off the gate control, we found a shallow area of the flume and jumped down, landing in about twenty-five centimetres of water. We then walked back up the flume to the control gate.

When we were nearly eight metres from the dam, the bottom of the flume began to slope down. Bob and I walked about another metre, and the water became nearly a metre deep. We were fully clothed, though, and not wanting to get any wetter, we both headed back to the shallower spot and climbed out.

Carmen walked another metre past where Bob and I had been, and the water there was almost one and a half metres deep. Satisfied, Carmen turned around and headed back out himself. By this time Bob and I were back up on the road that ran parallel to the flume. Seeing Carmen turn back, we urged him to go farther to make sure it would be deep enough.

He shrugged off our concern, saying it dropped one metre in depth with still nearly five metres in distance to go, and he figured he would have plenty of water to dive in at the slope of the flume bottom. We shrugged as well and said, "You're the one diving. It's your call."

Getting back onto the dam, Carmen was positioned and ready to dive. We gave one more protest: "Are you sure it will be deep enough?" "No problem. I'll do a shallow dive anyway." At that, he dove.

It was a perfect dive, unfortunately, for a diving competition—a perfect, straight-as-an-arrow entry. Carmen hit the bottom of the flume with both legs still a half-metre out of the water. If he had walked one more step when testing the depth he would have felt the flume bottom level at that point.

Jumping off the dam, Bob and I ran to the side of the flume. Carmen was holding his left hand over his face as the blood streamed down and through his fingers. We didn't help matters much by telling him what a stupid thing it was to do. "We warned you!" did not bring much relief after the fact. Blood continued to stream steadily from the gash on his forehead. I told him to keep his head in the cold water so that it might stop the bleeding. I wasn't sure if that was, in fact, correct, but the bleeding did slow down.

We helped him out of the flume and into the truck. I had a T-shirt that he held over his wound. It was a nasty gash but by the time we got out to the Gold River Highway, about twenty-six kilometres from Campbell River, the bleeding had stopped. We arrived at my place around suppertime.

When we got out of the truck, my fourteen-year-old brother Les, who was living with me at the time, came to ask if we had gotten a bear. Bob said, "We sure did! In fact Carmen got him, or at least the bear got Carmen."

Les's eyes got wide. "What?" he said. Carmen turned to show the ugly gash on his face and the large amount of dried blood still on his cheek and neck. Les came unhinged. "No! Really? Where is the bear now?" To which we replied, "Probably still up there somewhere, waiting for someone else to maul. Lucky we scared the bear off, but we couldn't kill him."

To this day Les has never been told otherwise.

* * *

A side note to this story: two years later, while hunting in the same area with Les, I shot a large black bear. The bear was about a hundred metres up a hill. I shot and it dropped stone dead. Les, still thinking about the "bear attack" on Carmen, was too petrified to leave the safety of the truck.

Finally I convinced him to join me because I needed his help to dress and skin the bear. I approached it until I was only about a metre away. Les, still scared shitless about ten metres away, kept asking me to confirm that the bear was dead.

"Is he dead?" "Yes, he is." "Are you sure?" "Yes, I'm sure!"

Gingerly, he approached, with me taunting him a bit for being so scared. "What do you want me to do?" he asked, his voice breaking.

"Hold his back legs while I turn him over to gut."

Les grabbed the back legs, I grabbed the right front leg and as I jerked the bear to its back, it let out a low moan as air escaped the hole in its chest. Les screamed and did a backwards jump in the air that would have been a world-record standing jump. Ten minutes later I finally convinced him that the bear was surely dead.

I think the Carmen story might have been the single biggest traumatic event of Les's life. I need to ask him about that.

The Code

Sometimes in life you need to pick your battles—if you can. Unfortunately, that is not always possible. Back in 1981 was one of those times when I had no choice, or at least I did not believe I did.

I worked for a strip joint/night club called JJ's in downtown Campbell River. It was not a high-class drinking establishment by any means. I worked there as a bouncer. It was common to be involved in altercations almost nightly but for the most part they were short-lived skirmishes that were brought under control fairly quickly, whether I was working alone or in conjunction with the other bouncers. Most nights there were three of us on the floor.

This particular night was one of those nights when maybe I should have picked my battle. Earlier in the day, before I was to come on shift at 6:00 p.m., I decided to head up to McIvor Lake to do a little fishing. I arrived at the turnoff to the lake and drove in partway, only to be met by four Hells Angels at the park gate. I stopped in front of the gate as two of them walked around the gate toward me. I asked what the problem was, and was told that the park was closed for a private function.

Surprised, I said, "Since when?" One of the bikers replied, "Since yesterday, got a problem with that?" I said, "I do, but I guess it doesn't matter." I turned my truck around and headed back home. When I reached the highway again, there were now two marked police vehicles turning back people who also wanted to head to the lake.

I pulled up alongside one of the officers and asked, "What the hell is going on? How can I be stopped from going in to the lake?" The cop told me that it was exclusively for the use of the Hells Angels for what is known as "Angel Acres." They would be using the campground for three more days and until then it would be closed to the public. I continued on my way, a little pissed, but resigned that that was how it was going to be.

At 6:00 p.m. I arrived at JJ's to start my evening shift. There would be four of us on that night, as it was extremely busy in town because of the BC Day long weekend. The other bouncers on that night were Randy, Doug and Norm. Norm was a gutless little weasel who was known to hide at the first sign of an altercation.

I was the head doorman that night. My job was to keep the numbers in the bar within fifty of the posted fire regulations (we were often way over). More importantly, I was to keep out anyone who I considered to be a threat to the safety of other bar patrons. The work was usually stressful later at night regardless of who ended up inside.

For the first few hours, even though we were packed, it was a pretty calm night. A few situations arose, but nothing that couldn't be quelled and controlled fairly quickly. That was about to change as three Hells Angels came through the first set of doors and stepped into the bar.

Our policies stated that no knives were permitted, and neither was the wearing of colours. Colours identified your gang affiliation. I stood in front of the three bikers and asked them to turn their vests inside out to hide their colours and to hand in their knives, which I would put behind the bar for safekeeping until they were ready to leave.

The biker closest to me proudly showed me his tattoo, which signified his membership with the Satan's Choice organization, apparently an affiliate of the Hells Angels. "This is my pass to go where I want to go, when I want," he said, "so you can just f— off!" I replied, "Nice tat, but you're not coming in regardless."

At that moment one of his two buddies tried to brush past me. I placed my hand on the buddy's chest and said, "Sorry, bro, you're not coming in until you hide the colours and give me your knives." The fellow stopped pushing, and I thought the situation might be under control. But as I turned back to face the tattooed biker, he hit me with a sucker punch to the side of my head. I shook it off and grabbed him in a headlock, sweeping his legs and tripping him onto his back. He hit the floor hard with me on top. I continued to hold him in a death-grip headlock out of fear and anger for being suckered.

As we lay on the floor, I could see two sets of size-twelve Daytons on either side of me. I waited for the kicks to my head to start, as was usually the case in previous altercations with more than one assailant. But neither of the floored biker's companions did a thing. They both simply stood there the whole time I had this guy down. I found out later that he was supposed to be the vice-president of a chapter of the Hells Angels. He just kept saying for me to let him up. I agreed to do that if he was prepared to comply or drink elsewhere.

He finally agreed so I let him back up. But as soon as he was on his feet again he took another swing at me. I dodged the blow, grabbed him by the throat with both hands and bent him backwards over a railing that ran about three metres along either side of the entrance inside the bar.

He again voiced his displeasure, telling me to "Stop this f—in' BS." Then, quite surprisingly, he exclaimed that this was embarrassing. I again told him, a little more forcefully as I pushed hard on his throat, that I would let him go if he and his buddies would leave. There were plenty of other places to go and drink. He agreed again, so I pushed off and took a step back. No sooner did I do that than he came at me once again. By this time I had had enough.

I straight-armed him with both hands on his throat again, but this time I aimed his head for the sharp edge of the open door jamb. He hit with a resounding thud before dropping to his knees like he was shot. He lay there half conscious. After a few moments his two large buddies grabbed an arm each, hoisted him up and half dragged him out the fire door. They continued out through the main doors until they disappeared.

I followed to make sure there was not going to be another episode, at least not in the club. By this time my so-called support crew of Doug, Randy and Norm had shown up, and they now stood with me at the entrance doors. The three Hells Angels were on the sidewalk in front of the entrance where their bikes were parked. The VP, still a bit groggy and bleeding from the back of his head, pointed to each of the other bouncers and told them, without qualification, that they were a bunch of pussies, then pointed at me and said, "But this guy's got balls!" They saddled up and away they went. The adrenaline was still flowing hard through my veins, but after a few minutes I calmed down.

Apparently Robert, the bartender, had phoned the police when the first altercation started. The detachment was only a minute or two from our club, but they didn't show up until about two minutes after the Hells Angels left. It was as if they'd been hiding around the corner, waiting for them to leave. They showed as much courage as my chickenshit backup bouncers who couldn't be found until the Angels were out of the club!

The rest of the night went without a hitch. When a little situation arose between two patrons, I walked over and shook my finger at them and they sat down promptly and behaved the rest of the night.

At 2:30 a.m. I left the club, now closed, and headed for my place. I lived in a big house that I was renting across from the oceanfront. I lived there alone as I was going through a divorce from my first wife and would not have custody of my sons for another couple of years.

As I drove into the yard some things didn't look quite right. I parked my truck and walked up to the front step to find my door was not fully closed. Lights were on that shouldn't have been and a light was off that should have been on. It didn't take long for my thoughts to turn back to the events that took place earlier in the night.

I had left a large glass pop bottle sitting on my step. I picked it up, pushed open the door and waited for what I thought was going to be payback for my earlier actions. As I entered, nothing jumped out at me. I continued on through the house, checking each room. They were all empty, but I knew someone had been there or still was. I was a creature of habit and followed a prescribed ritual in regard to lights and closing my door.

The last room I checked was my bedroom, the door of which I left open in the summer so it stayed somewhat cooler. It was now mostly shut. I pushed the door open slowly. When it was half open I jumped in, brandishing my glass pop bottle and letting out a yell, more out of terror than confidence.

I was relieved—and a bit embarrassed—to find the room empty! It was a very fitful sleep that night, but by the light of the morning sun shining through my living room window, I felt that if retribution was coming, it would have been executed by now.

There is an unwritten code, I believe, even among criminal elements, that respect is given to those who do not show cowardice. Let me make this perfectly clear: at no time was I not feeling fear from the fight of the night before, but I have always felt that if you're in the right, you will usually have the upper hand.

Later on in the day, I was talking with my friend Bob. I told him of the happenings the previous night and about my front door being open and the lights on and all the extra drama it created.

Bob, a little chagrined, apologetically informed me that he and Darrell, another buddy of mine, had come by and used my sauna and had a couple of beers. I had an open-door policy for my friends and they were welcome to come on in anytime. However, I made it very well understood that, from then on, they had to leave my place exactly how they found it!

Sucker Punch

Hockey can be a rough sport, and it was especially so back in the 1970s and the era of the Broad Street Bullies, a.k.a. the Philadelphia Flyers. You expected a hockey game at some point to have two players, or even two entire teams, square off in battle.

It was early October 1974, and my team had just won a fun and action-packed game in Comox at Glacier Gardens. I was nineteen years old and had played a spirited game, and I was feeling the effects. I showered up and shortly after 10:00 p.m. was on my way back home to Campbell River with my first wife, Lynne, our baby boy, Kelly Jr., and a young friend of ours, Debbie. I was feeling pretty good. I'd had a good game and took the victory as well earned.

As we were getting close to home, the rain started to lightly fall, carrying on through Willow Point and along the coast highway, which then followed the waterfront all the way to town. I could see the Big Rock store off to our left along the straight stretch that passed by what is now Rotary Park.

Suddenly, standing in front of us, seemingly out of nowhere, was this big dude dressed in black with his right hand stuck out to the side, indicating he was hitchhiking, and his left hand raised, palm out, as if to stop us. I swerved into the oncoming lane to keep from hitting him, instantly angry. He could have cost us our lives if another vehicle had been coming, or he himself could have been killed. I pulled to the side of the road as the fellow charged up to my vehicle, saying, "Thanks, man."

Jumping out of the car, I told him I hadn't stopped to give him a ride but to tell him he was an idiot and could have got someone killed. Clearly that wasn't what he wanted to hear. "Go f— yourself!" he spat back at me in a sudden rage.

I took off my jacket and threw it through the half-open driver's window, telling Lynne, "Someone needs a lesson taught." I turned back to face the guy just in time to receive a sucker punch to the side of my head. I could feel my legs start to give out a bit. He was a big dude, as I mentioned, and probably had twenty kilos on me.

Through my somewhat blurry vision, I could see another haymaker coming from the left side. I ducked the blow and his momentum carried him almost full circle. My adrenaline was pumping and as my head started to clear, I was able to get him in a rear choke. Dragging him behind the car, I did a leg sweep and he fell hard to the wet pavement. I warned him to never do that kind of shit again. I turned to go back to the driver's door and as I reached for the door handle, Debbie yelled, "Watch out!"

Whirling around, I saw another haymaker coming, but this time Debbie's warning gave me enough time to throw a counter left hook, catching him flush on the top of his right cheekbone. This time he staggered a little. I threw a solid straight right then grabbed him by his coat and pushed him back behind the car again. My momentum knocked him over backwards. As soon as he hit the ground I was on him, no mercy or warnings to be given anymore.

I hit him four or five times about the head, then stood and kicked him in the ribs and head. He tried a couple of times to get from his hands and knees to his feet, but I kept punching him in the face. I could see blood running from his face profusely as the taillights of my car illuminated the ground behind the vehicle. Tiring from hitting him in an awkward bent-over position, I stood up fully again. He tried to get to his feet but he was weaving back and forth, unable to pull up a leg enough to stand.

I told him again that he was warned. Then, taking one more well-aimed and forceful kick, I caught him under his chin, snapping his head back completely. He collapsed; not a muscle moved. All I could see was blood pooling heavily and glistening in the taillights. I waited for another fifteen seconds or so to see if there was any movement. There was none. Panicking, I jumped back in the car and sped away.

Getting to our house after dropping off Debbie, I quickly unloaded my hockey gear before collapsing on the couch in absolute fear that I might have just killed someone. The next two days were like hell for me. I listened to the local radio station, checked the newspapers—anything that might report the happenings of that fateful night. I heard nothing.

The third day found me in the dressing room with the other senior men's hockey team I played for. As I sat in the dressing room suiting up for the game, I heard one of our players talking about this guy he'd seen in the bank earlier in the day, and how it looked like the fellow had been hit by a train. His face was completely black and blue and swollen to twice its normal size.

He went on further, saying that if it wasn't a train there must one tough mofo who laid a hell of a beating on him because this guy was one tough dude himself. Some of the players seemed to know the guy; their description seemed familiar. I asked a few questions about who he was and what he looked like. It was the same guy I had fought, that was certain.

I said nothing, but when the final buzzer went at the end of a two-to-one final for our team, I was relieved for getting the win, but far more relieved that I had not killed another human being. My short fuse has always been a weakness of mine over the years, but maturity and a dedicated wife have helped me improve. May it continue!

Once Was More Than Enough

I have been an avid outdoorsman and hunter since I was sixteen years old. Every winter I read hunting magazines cover to cover, rent hunting videos and basically can never get enough days afield, whether through books, videos or in real life. Bears are probably my favourite game animals to hunt. I've usually found them to be plentiful on Vancouver Island, where I lived for a good portion of my life.

While in conversation with a couple of hunters prior to the 1977 hunting season, I was asked if I would consider guiding one of them on what would be his first bear hunt. I had taken a few different fellows out over the past few years with good success.

My hunter's name was Rob. He passed away many years ago, but I know this hunt was a hunting highlight of his life. He may have called it something other than a highlight, though.

I decided to go up to Bear Lake (also known as McCreight Lake). It was aptly named as the old logging slashes situated above and north of the lake held some good bear populations. Berries covering the hillsides were a plentiful food source for bears looking to fatten themselves up for the winter months. Early fall bears, having fed on blueberries and huckleberries all summer, are probably the nicest wild game fare there is. Moose and elk are a close second.

Driving up the old and nearly washed-out road that ran up the mountain, we soon entered the beginning of the logged area. We pulled over to park and went by foot the rest of the way.

It had been daylight for well over an hour, but that was not too critical because this area got little hunting pressure so the bears were content to feed until mid-morning on most days. Days like today, which started crisp and cool with clear blue skies, were especially good for feeding. Another asset was the breeze, which gently blew directly into our faces.

Rob was shooting a .270-calibre rifle. I was carrying my trusty and deadly .30-06, and using 180-grain Noslers. After thirty minutes we came around a corner of the road that led to the west side of the mountain overlooking Bear Lake.

"There, up there!" I half whispered to Rob, pointing to a large bear on the opposite hillside. It was about three hundred metres away. I lay across a large stump on the side of the road to get a better read on its size and quality. Zooming in my Bushnell scope on the feeding bear, I could see it was indeed exceptional. Its hide was lustrous, long and even. I judged that it was in excess of 185 kilos and squared almost two metres. This was a nice bear!

Rob was impatiently asking me, "Can I take it?" I answered, "It's a great-looking bear. Yes!" Rob quickly dropped to the ground behind the same stump I had just been using to judge the bear's size and quality. I asked him what he was doing. He anxiously replied, "I'm going to shoot it!"

"Whoa! Hold on!" I said. "It's a very long shot. It's also a big bear. I want no chance of wounding him." Once before, I had tracked an even larger bear carrying five 180-grain slugs in it, and I was not about to repeat that experience. As he protested and asked me to let him shoot from where we were, I assured him the bear was oblivious to us. The wind was in our favour and we would have good cover once we started the stalk. He reluctantly agreed.

We hurried along until we were within what I surmised was about seventy metres. The only problem was we were at the bottom of a small hill that blocked our view of the bear's location. Confident that it was still in the same place, I climbed the hill to below where it was feeding. I removed my boots just before the top so as to be as quiet as possible. I knew he would be close when I crested the hill. Rob did the same, following right behind me.

As I reached high enough to see beyond the hill, there he was, feeding, only about thirty metres away. He was broadside to me and still completely unaware of our presence.

I motioned with my right hand for Rob to carefully position himself beside me for a clear shot. Once alongside me, he too saw the bear. Judging by the look on his face, the bear had seemingly grown much larger than it had looked when we first spotted it.

Rob, using hand signals, asked me again if the shoulder shot was the shot to take. I nodded in the affirmative. Just as I nodded, the wind swirled and was blowing directly at this huge bear. I expected the bear to bolt. It did not.

Rob was trying to steady himself for the shot. The bear continued to be seemingly unaware of our presence. Strange, I thought. Bears have a remarkably acute sense of smell, and with the wind blowing directly toward it, I figured surely it knew we were there and what we were. But the bear just kept looking away. However, I noticed that it was opening and closing its mouth against the huckleberry bush it had been feeding on but was not actually eating anything, almost like it was just going through the motions.

Rob took a deep breath and fired. The bullet struck its mark perfectly, square in the shoulder. Then it happened. In a split second the bear came running at us in a full-out charge. No bluff, but the real deal! I saw the frothy spit shoot from its mouth as it roared its malicious intent.

I raised my .30-06 only to see nothing but black in my scope. I had neglected to turn the scope back down to three power, which I would normally do when getting that close to any bear. All I could see now was a solid black, charging menace at nine-power magnification. Rob continued to fire, still in his prone position. I, likewise, kept firing. The bear, undaunted, stayed true to its unswerving purpose. It had payback and vengeance on its mind.

The bear was now within four metres. I dropped my gun to my hip and fired. The bear nosedived and spun off to our right but as fast as it went down, it was up and carrying on. Thankfully it went in the other direction but in doing so passed both of us close enough to touch with the barrel of our guns. It went over the hill and we lost sight of it. We waited and hoped it would succumb to its wounds. Rob was shaking and white as a ghost. I was only slightly better.

Suddenly, on the opposite hillside, our bear appeared, still running as if it was not injured at all. My clip was empty. Rob had one shot left. As the bear was about to crest the opposite hill 140 metres away and continue on down the other side, Rob fired his last bullet. It was a perfect brain shot. The bear tumbled forty metres down the hill then with one last tumble it laid lifeless. We watched the fallen bear for five minutes and finally felt confident that it was dead. We hurried over, excited to see this large bear up close, and it was every bit as big or even bigger than we'd first surmised.

I began to dress the bear. I was curious why it did not drop instantly after Rob's well-placed shot, and I wanted to see how many more slugs it had taken. I skinned it back enough to see only two places where it had been hit other than the final head shot that finished it off. Rob's first bullet, a 160-grain Sierra Boat Tail, was lodged just inside the massive front shoulder. It had mushroomed nicely but done no real damage or even penetrated into the muscle very far. My last shot from the hip, at point-blank range, had struck it just along the top of its muscular shoulder—enough to force him down, but not enough to be a mortal shot either, as neither the vitals nor the spine were hit.

The bear did measure a full two metres, outstretched. I guessed its weight to be right where I'd originally judged it to be, maybe a bit closer to two hundred kilos and possibly as much as 215. The front paws were over fifteen centimetres wide with the toes closed.

Rob was thrilled with the outcome, although he reminded me how much easier and less terrifying it would have been to shoot it from three hundred metres when we first spotted it.

I simply replied, "What would be the joy in that?"

Rob never again asked to go bear hunting. In his words, once was more than enough!

Van in Orbit

What started out as just another rainy spring day on Vancouver Island would turn into one of the most frightening, unbelievable days of my life.

I was seventeen years old and working as a mechanic and welder's apprentice for a logging company out near Roberts Lake, approximately twenty-two kilometres north of Campbell River. Lynne and I and the kids lived in Stories Beach, south of town, which made it a thirty-five-kilometre drive every day. At that time I had no vehicle of my own, so I was given an old '56 Chev panel van to commute to work each day. This truck was not the greatest vehicle or the safest, but it was in keeping with a widely held truism among mechanics: everyone else's vehicle ran great because of your expertise, but yours was a piece of junk held together with wire and duct tape. The passenger's-side front brakes had a tendency to lock up when trying to stop, pulling the van hard to the right. It was much more pronounced if trying to stop abruptly.

Lynne and I were heading into Campbell River early one evening to do some grocery shopping. As we neared the city, rain was coming down quite heavily. Somewhere between Third and Fifth Avenue, I noticed two young men, perhaps in their mid-twenties, standing on the opposite side of the highway from us, on the west side. The east side was a fairly abrupt drop-off to the ocean some thirty metres below. They appeared to be contemplating crossing the highway to the ocean side.

When we were about thirty to forty metres away, doing around fifty-five kilometres per hour, without warning they decided to cross in front of us. Fearing a collision, I slammed on the brakes and immediately the panel van jerked violently toward the road's shoulder, with the young men frantically running in the very same direction we were skidding.

Suddenly they both disappeared in front of us. Moments later we came to a stop. In horror, I got out to see if I had just run them both over. As I opened my door I hit the power pole to my left. I looked straight down to see one of the young men crawling up the bank directly below my vehicle. He was cursing at me because I could have killed them both. Arriving on the shoulder of the bank, he continued on down the highway toward town. I noticed that his friend had now joined him and seemed to be relatively okay, although they were still swearing and looking back and making plenty of hand gestures in my direction.

I closed my door, shaking both from adrenaline and relief that I had indeed not run them over. As I started the van, I noticed that six or more cars had stopped and their occupants were staring at us in what seemed to be disbelief. Maybe they were as surprised as we were that we had not killed the young men. I put the van in gear, drove back out onto the road and we continued on our way.

The next day while heading to work, I couldn't help but think about what had transpired the day before. Still a little shaken up, I neared the place where it had happened. At the exact location, I noticed a set of skid marks in the gravel on the shoulder of the road, indicating where the strange occurrence had unfolded.

What I observed next was beyond bizarre and beyond any reason that the laws of physics or common sense could explain. Pulling the van over to the side of the road, I went to investigate further. There was the power pole I'd nearly hit. And there were two tire tracks—still visible even after the rain—heading for the pole and leading over the edge of the cliff. But on the drop-off side of the power pole, there was only a single tire track. The power pole was only a metre from the edge of the cliff, which meant the van's outside wheel must have been suspended in midair. The van had somehow defied gravity and all logic and reason. One could argue that I'd imagined the whole event, but the forensics proved irrefutable.

I had indeed experienced something that could never be explained by science or logic—but it happened. This I know with surety.

I have my conclusion; you can choose yours!

Way Too Close for Comfort

Every summer, I looked forward to going to one of my all-time favourite fishing spots, Eve River, situated in the north-east part of Vancouver Island. The weather in mid-June usually consists of warm, sun-filled days with just enough of an offshore breeze to keep the bugs away. This particular day my oldest son, Brent, and I left early in the morning to enjoy a day of fishing and do a little early hunting-season scouting. At ten years old, Brent was already an ardent and experienced outdoorsman and soon would become a consistent hunting companion. Archery hunting season would start in the latter part of August.

The day started out fairly uneventfully, but it was about to change for Brent and me. Just over one and a half hours after leaving Campbell River, we reached the logging road turnoff that would bring us out to the estuary at Eve River. We had not gone far when, rounding a corner on the road, we startled a blacktail doe; it quickly jumped off the road. I was so intent on missing the doe, now standing on the bank, that I narrowly missed its fawn, lying smack-dab in the middle of the road.

Slamming on the brakes, I came to a stop only a few centimetres away from the fawn. It was late in the year for such a young fawn, which I guessed to be no more than two or three days old. It must have been a very late drop. Both Brent and I jumped out of the truck, hoping to find that we had not killed the fawn. Thankfully, the little sweetheart was okay.

She continued to lie perfectly still on the road with her front feet placed strategically over her eyes in a kind of "if I can't see you, then you can't see me" understanding. The mother had now moved farther off the road but continued to watch with a great deal of concern. We tried to scare the fawn off the road, but it would not even remotely respond to us kicking our feet in the gravel or our loud encouragement to get off the road. We both agreed that if we tried to drive around her, she might inadvertently move at the last second and be run over.

Finally, Brent reached down and picked the fawn up in his arms. At first the little girl's heart was pounding fast, but almost immediately she calmed down, then began to lick Brent's ear and cheek. He cuddled the little deer for a few moments before I suggested we put her off the road with her mother.

The mother never stopped watching us. Brent placed the fawn up on the top of the bank where the doe was standing, only five metres or so away from her. As soon as we backed away, and contrary to the nonsense about how if you touch a fawn the mother will abandon it, the fawn's momma came rushing over to her young one. She began to vigorously lick her from top to bottom and continued until she felt that her child was sufficiently free of that awful human smell. The mother and her little one ambled off, none the worse for wear, never giving Brent or me a second glance.

Back in the truck, we were anxious to get on our way and get some great fishing in. Twenty minutes later we were parked just up from the log dump for the Eve River Logging Company. We unloaded our gear and made haste for the mouth of the estuary, where the first few pink salmon would be showing up. A bonus would be the chance to catch some really nice sea-run Dolly Varden trout, which could weigh up to one and a half kilos. We hiked down through the dry tidal flats and out to the mouth of the river.

The tide was nearly all the way out. The salmon fishing would begin to get good as the tide flooded back in. Brent and I would have about two to three hours of great fishing, before the tide would push us upriver and off the tidal flats. That would be plenty of time to get all the fishing action we could handle. We both fished for about an hour and caught and released about five or six fish. After that, Brent, being a ten-year-old, was getting a little bored of catching fish. (Is that even possible?) He decided he was just going to lie up on the beach by an old root that had washed down during the spring flood.

I continued fishing, standing about hip-deep in water. I needed the extra distance as I stood on the edge of the sheer drop-off where the sea-run Dollies were cruising back and forth. They were waiting to feed on the eggs of the pink salmon that were also starting to mill up in the mouth of the river. Shortly after Brent went up the beach, I began to hook into Dollies one after another. Catching two really nice-sized ones, I called out to Brent to meet me halfway along the beach to retrieve them for me. I didn't want to stop fishing. He hollered, "Sure."

I waded in toward the shore. As I reached where the water was about knee-deep, Brent met me, took the two nice trout and headed back to his stump on the shore.

All morning we had seen a few bald eagles flying about and perched in a tree opposite the riverbank. As I headed back to my fishing, I hadn't gone more than ten metres when I heard an eagle screech very close by. I felt the urge to turn back to Brent. Coming down at a full dive was a large eagle, talons outstretched, now less than a metre from my son. I screamed as loud as I could, "Brent, watch out!"

Brent turned to see the eagle on him. He threw his hands above his head to protect himself, still holding the fish. The eagle banked hard, only centimetres from his head, and grabbed the trout out of his left hand. Brent said later that he could feel the wind and force of the eagle's wings as it snatched the fish. With a mighty beat of its wings the raptor flew away, only to have the fish slip from its grasp and fall into the river. Brent looked back at me as he sat on the rocky beach, drew his hands across his brow, then smiled a large but uncomfortable grin of relief.

You would think that was more than enough excitement for one day but it was nowhere near over yet. I had at least forty-five minutes left before the tide would push us off the flats. Seeing a few salmon start to roll and surface, I hurried out to the drop-off. The water was now almost up to my lower chest, but for me to be able to cast to the salmon that were cruising the mouth of the river, I needed to be right on the edge of the drop-off. The depth dropped to nearly fifty metres at this point.

I threw one cast after another but the salmon and Dolly Vardens were not co-operating at all. I was thinking it might still be too early in the year for the run to really heat up, and besides, the tide was almost mid-chest. I decided to make a few more quick casts and then it would be time to go.

Strangely, above the ocean breeze and the lapping of the waves, I thought I could hear someone crying. I strained hard to listen, even looked back at Brent, now with thirty-plus metres of water between us. He just waved and smiled. Again, I could hear a whining kind of cry. Bewildered and curious, I stood still, trying to identify the origin of the sound. Suddenly, the fin of a massive killer whale surfaced within four metres of me, and it was followed by another seven or eight whales in the pod—they were feeding only a few metres away.

I scrambled to get away from the drop-off. The water was now so high that I became very buoyant and my feet could barely touch the sea bottom. In sheer terror I thrashed about to reach a safe place, using a kind of backstroke to pull myself away from the feeding frenzy that was going on. Finally getting some traction, I kept pulling with my arms and pushing with my heels to get into shallow water. I had seen killer whales grab seals from as little as half a metre of water. I kept thinking that at any moment I was going to be grabbed by my legs and dragged out to a painful and hideous death. Frantically, I tried to get more traction on the silty bottom.

At last reaching shore, I fell onto the beach and tried to calm my breathing and my pounding heartbeat. Brent had been walking the beach to try fishing upriver so he was unaware of what had happened, only seeing me crash on the beach in complete exhaustion when he happened to look back.

Yes, truly this was a day that would never be forgotten. Every vivid detail from the sweet innocence of the morning, the drama and close call of the earlier part of the day and the absolute terror of my last few moments in the water would be etched in my mind forever. Thank God for an uneventful, thoroughly incident-free and welcome trip home!

Fighting for My Mother's Life

My mother, Rose, suffered through a difficult marriage to my father, Bruce, for sixteen long years. She had been abused in most every conceivable way. I witnessed this when I was as young as five years of age. Violence, as you might have realized by now from my other stories, was a large part of what was present in our home and lives.

We moved from our home in Campbell River when I was only nine years old— me, my parents and my seven siblings. It was 1964. Initially, my father moved with us to our new home on DeHart Road in Kelowna. That was the last time I can remember my dad being at home with us, other than the odd visit, which included Christmas for the next couple of years. I was not aware that my father and mother were actually on the verge of divorce. I could tell a vast story about the years between this time in my life and the events I want to share now, but I will skip it and fast-track to the twelfth year of my life.

At that time my mother was able to purchase a lot on Findlay Road in Rutland, a hamlet just a few miles east of downtown Kelowna. It was considered a low-rent district and had a large smattering of orchards and a couple of vineyards. We built our home with the help of my uncles and soon, as summer came to an end and the house was livable, we were back in school.

Around this time drug and alcohol use became prevalent in our home. My older brothers Robin, Sandy and Terry were still living with us but it was more of a home base to party, or eat, sleep and clean up. They spent little time in the house other than that. My mom had been living with a man named Harvey for about two years, and they would marry one year later.

Harvey was quite a bit younger than my mother and was anything but a father figure; however, I tried to see him as one. We had not been in this new home for long before the violence and abuse began again, only to become more frequent. I will not go into the sexual or emotional abuse that was happening at this time, but will instead focus on the violence that took place.

Regularly I witnessed violent altercations with Harvey's mother and sister ganging up on my mom, but mostly the violence was carried out against my mother by Harvey. Many a night would find me and sometimes my younger sister Penny defending our mother against the beatings he would inflict on her. In some cases my mother had to be hospitalized.

One terrifying night stands out in my memory as clear as if it was happening at this very moment. I had just turned fourteen. Mom and Harvey arrived home around midnight from a night of partying. Not long after they entered the house, the yelling and arguing started. I lay in my bed, angry and scared for what I knew would transpire as it had on so many other nights.

As the argument escalated, the sounds of furniture being tipped over and punches and kicks being thrown increased. As the fight became more violent, I got angrier. I heard my mother being thrown hard against a wall. The screams told me she was once again in mortal danger. Harvey was capable of that sort of violence, especially when alcohol was combined with the drugs he was currently taking.

My brother Sandy had a .22 rifle that was stored under the stairwell, a space that also served as a makeshift closet for me and my two younger brothers, Les and Lory. Jumping from my bed, I grabbed the .22, found the box of shells and loaded the single-shot Cooey.

As I entered the living room, standing near the dining room entrance was my stepfather with my mother's arms held behind her back and a twenty-centimetre butcher knife held to her throat. In a trembling voice, I mustered all the courage I could, raised the rifle and aimed it at Harvey's head. I demanded that he drop the knife and let my mom go. He challenged me, sarcastically saying I didn't have the guts and that if I didn't drop the gun he would slit her throat. I could feel my body responding to the terror I was feeling for my mother and myself.

The standoff seemed like it went on for minutes when in reality it was only a few seconds. Suddenly, Harvey threw my mom to the floor and lunged at me. I did not know if he had dropped the knife, but as he reached for me I quickly ejected the shell from the rifle, truly believing that if he'd gotten the gun from me, he would have shot me dead.

Harvey pinned me to the floor and began to choke me. He was a six-foot-tall logger who worked as a faller (when he worked) and was far stronger than me, especially when enraged. I struggled to pry his vice-like grip from my throat, to no avail. I felt myself losing consciousnesses when suddenly, as I was about to pass out, his grip loosened and he fell to the floor beside me. I gasped for air and rolled away from him as he was trying to get back up.

As my head cleared I saw my sister Penny holding a cast-iron frying pan in her trembling hands and knew that she had more than likely just saved my life. As we ran back to our bedrooms, I waited for what I thought would be a retaliation. After an hour of huddled fear I climbed into bed, and I heard nothing for the rest of that sleepless night.

Harvey took great pleasure in inflicting pain on all of us small children, especially me. I won't talk of the horrors he perpetrated on my sisters. I don't feel I have the right to do so.

Another memory of what he was capable of is also still as clear as the day it happened. I was caught smoking, something all the older brothers and adults did in our home. Nonetheless, I was to be punished and Harvey was to carry out the sentence.

In my sisters' room were bunk beds. Harvey escorted me into the room and instructed me to kneel on the floor, reach across the metal-framed bed and grip the railing on the other side. I did as I was told for fear that the punishment would include being punched in the head if I didn't, which he was more than comfortable doing.

I closed my eyes, face down on the bed, and felt the first biting sting. The pain was the most intense I had ever felt. I had been strapped before, but this was far more painful. Again I felt an intense, burning pain across my upper legs. I wanted to let go and run but I knew it would be futile and only exacerbate the situation. Penny was outside the room and heard my cries of pain. She counted the blows, which numbered twenty-one.

Finally exhausted, Harvey stopped. I reached back to feel my burning legs and buttocks, believing it was over, and felt moisture saturating my pants. When I brought my hand forward, it was covered in blood. I turned to face Harvey. He was smiling at me, and in his hands was the bloodstained tea kettle cord. For days I could not fully bend my legs until the swelling eventually subsided and the pain began to lessen.

After a number of similar skirmishes, it would come to an end seven months later, at least as far as Harvey and I were concerned. I had just fallen asleep one night; I'm not sure of the time. Suddenly I was awakened to voices yelling outside our house and a vehicle still running. I stood on my bed and peered out the window.

In the driveway was my mother's Galaxy, parked about three metres from the front steps. Mom and Harvey were yelling at each other again, as usual. My mother was in the driver's seat. After a minute or so she opened the door and stepped out. Approaching the front steps, she was now positioned between the house and the car. Harvey slid across to the driver's seat, put the car in gear and accelerated toward my mom. He narrowly missed her as the car collided with the foundation wall of the house.

He jumped from the car and dove across the hood, grabbing at my mom as she tried to run up the porch steps. Unfortunately he caught her leg, which slowed her down long enough for him to reach up and grab her by the hair. Pulling her off the top step to the ground below, he pinned her down and was punching her repeatedly about the face and head as she struggled to deflect the blows. I jumped from my bed and raced outside.

When I got there, I tripped and fell by the small rock fence that lined our driveway. Picking up one of the rocks, about the size of a melon, I charged toward Harvey, who was still focused on the beating he was inflicting on my mom. I drove the rock hard into the top right side of his head. He slumped forward, the blood already visible in the porch light as it poured from a gaping wound. Unbelievably, he jumped up and turned his attention on me.

I ran up onto the porch deck with Harvey in pursuit. My sister Penny held the door open. I burst through the front door and, fearing Harvey was gaining on me, continued right out the back door, heading for the back fence and a farmer's field behind our place. After clearing the fence I looked back and found that he was no longer pursuing me. In fact, according to my sister, he only got as far as the porch then staggered down the road leading to Highway 97 and on to Kelowna.

This was our last encounter of this sort. I left home a couple weeks later when advised to do so by my mother. I got my first job that very same day, in Christian Valley, BC, near Beaverdell. Being told to leave may have been what saved my life.

I relate this story with no animosity toward my mother or Harvey, may they rest in peace. It is simply to give understanding to who I am and what may have shaped some of my character traits, both good and bad. I have long ago forgiven them, including my father, Bruce. I know that if I could not have done so I would still feel the biting pain, anguish and sorrow that these events once caused.

Sometimes in life these pivotal moments may seem like the worst thing ever to happen. However, I believe that if we don't let them consume us, they truly can provide strength and empathy for both victims and perpetrators.

A Bear in Hand Is Worth Two in the Bush

Hunting has always provided me and my family with good wild-game meat for the freezer, although sometimes a lot more than bargained for. This particular outing to Bear Lake, one of my favourite locations for finding large black bears, found me and my hunting companion, Bob, glassing a decent-sized bear. Just 250 metres away from us, a young bear was feeding slowly along an old logging spur where succulent huckleberries and blueberries lined the ditches and hillside.

I had chosen to hunt with my archery gear that day. Even though it was rifle season, I loved to hunt with my bow. The challenge of getting close enough to a wild bear to execute a clean and fatal shot took some skill, not to mention the element of danger it would generate. Alas, when you're young and foolish you don't think about consequences as much as you do about the accomplishment and excitement.

The bear was making its way along the old spur, and feeling that I had ample time, I planned out a course of action for us. Bob was going to stay behind to watch the stalk from his vantage point, which was nearly forty metres higher than the bear. He would have a good field of view. I, on the other hand, would lose sight of the bear for the last seventy-five metres, but I could glass back at Bob. He would give me updates on the bear's movement and the distance I would be from it.

As fast and quietly as possible, I closed the distance between myself and Mr. Bruin. I made good time and when I looked back at Bob's location up on the hill, I could see by his hand signals that our bear had not moved much at all.

Feeling confident, I carried on. As I approached what I believed was the last corner of the spur that led to my quarry, I looked back one last time at Bob. When I glassed him on the hill, I could see him motioning to me that the bear was now only fifteen metres away and, in fact, just around the corner.

I nocked an arrow onto my sixty-pound Cobra compound bow before stealthily walking around the last corner.

Almost instantly, I was face to face with the bear at barely ten metres. We stared intently at each other, my right hand still holding my nocked arrow firmly in between my fingers. Wearing camouflage and with my face painted, I could see that the bear could not quite figure out what I was, if not dinner. I was barely breathing, afraid that it might trigger him into some sort of action. At that close range and facing me head-on, it would more than likely approach from the way it was facing if I tried a neck shot. That is not a bowhunter's best choice for a shot.

Slowly the bear turned away and walked up an old fir lying across a ditch. After going a metre or so up this log, it turned back to me. I had a quartering shot and it was now or never, as I felt it was about to bolt. I drew back fully, took a quick instinctive aim (I never used sights), then released the broadhead. The arrow entered the right side high on the lungs. The bear recoiled for a split second then charged up the log and out of sight over the ridge just in front of me.

I knew it was hit well and had to wait only fifteen minutes or so to be sure, then follow what would be a good blood trail.

Glassing back up to where Bob was, I gave the thumbs-up sign. But instead of seeing the reciprocal thumbs-up from him, I saw frantic waving, and what looked like motioning at something in front of me. I put my right palm out to the side in a questioning gesture, not understanding what all the panic was for.

In the same moment the reason for the panic became clear. Suddenly, over the ridge came what looked liked a very angry and determined bear. I hastily nocked another arrow and raised the bow. The bear continued toward me on an angle that would take it about ten metres in front of me and right across the logging spur. In fact that is what happened. I followed it across the road with my bow at full draw. It crossed the road and continued uninterrupted over the downhill side. I ran to the edge of the road just in time to see it drop lifeless as fast as it came into view just moments before. Relieved, I sat watching the motionless bear—I needed to wait until I felt assured that it was, in fact, dead. While I waited, I checked out where it had crossed the road and could see the frothy blood from the lung shot streaming across the road and as far as I could see down the hill. Yes, my bear was dead!

Leaving my bow and arrows on the road, I hurried down the hill to my trophy. This was my first black bear taken with archery gear, and no rifle backup either. When I reached it, I rolled it onto its back, pulled out my knife and started to dress it. I had no sooner started than I heard a coughing woof behind me. I knew instantly what had made the sound. I froze, unwilling or unable to move. Again I heard brush break and more soft woofing, kind of a nasally exhale. Looking down at my ten-centimetre lockback knife and feeling little comfort, I turned slowly but deliberately to face the end of what I thought could be my last hunting trip.

Four metres away stood another bear on its hind legs, testing the air to figure out what the heck was going on. Obviously, it could smell both the bear and me at that range. I turned until I faced it head-on, still on my knees. It kept standing on its hind legs and testing the air, unsure of what to do. It was so close I could actually see the confusion in its face. Finally, the young bear dropped down on all fours, let out another loud woof and was gone back into the thick timber below.

Finally Bob arrived, excited to see I was still alive. He related that he had witnessed the shot and knew the bear was hit. However, whereas I was unable to see the bear shortly after I shot, from his vantage point Bob could see the bear clearly. It had run about forty-five metres up the hill on the opposite side from where I was, then turned and headed back toward me.

From Bob's vantage point, it looked like the big guy had decided to come back to finish what I'd started, thus the frantic waving of his hands. When the bear crossed the road and I followed, Bob had lost sight of both of us and his imagination took over. He was relieved greatly that what he had imagined of the ensuing events was indeed just his imagination!

Man, That's Got to Hurt

The very first time for almost everything in life is fraught with mistakes, ignorance and/or Murphy's Law. Think about your first date, your first job, your first vehicle purchase...and the list goes on. Remember how many things went wrong, and in some cases, horribly wrong. The one thing most of us learned with all of those firsts was that we were not making those same mistakes again, ever! At least that was what we always promised ourselves.

Well, my first ever trip to Eureka Peak to hunt mule deer was also the first trip for my oldest sons, Kelly and Wade, as well as my long-time hunting buddy Bob from Vancouver Island. The plan was to leave Lone Butte right after I got off the evening shift at the welding and fabricating shop where I worked. I would be off work at 1:30 a.m., and we would immediately head out to Crooked Lake, a three-hour drive north of 100 Mile House. We would leave the vehicle up a mountain road as far as we could go, then carry on by foot with our packs loaded for a four-day hunt.

Just before work was finished, I saw Bob and the boys pull up out front with my F-150 extended cab 4×4. The truck was tired but still a good old truck. Pulling off my coveralls, I bid my friends at work good night and we were on our way. The mood was light and optimistic as we travelled along in the crisp early-morning air. We never passed a vehicle or even saw one all the way in to Crooked Lake.

We arrived at the base of the road that traversed steeply up the mountain bordering Crooked Lake on its east side. We were going to drive up as far as possible to decrease some of the hard climbing we would have to do with our heavy packs. We had only travelled about 250 metres up the steep mountain road when we were met by a large tree that had blown down.

It was far too big to move by hand, but I wasn't concerned as I had told Bob and the boys to bring my chainsaw to buck any limbs or trees that might be across the road. We all climbed out and I instructed Kelly to grab the saw. In the glow of the headlights I saw a perplexed look on his face. Again, I asked him to grab the saw. Sheepishly, he replied, "We forgot it."

"Now what are we going to do?" Bob asked with some concern. I shrugged and said, "Without a saw we're not going to drag a sixty-foot tree with that diameter off this road." I walked to the back of the truck and lifted the canopy door, hoping that by simply peering into the truck my chainsaw would magically appear. No such luck! I shone a flashlight around the pickup box and spotted, lying coiled up in my spare tire, a length of heavy jute rope that I kept in the truck for emergency tows for myself and others when out four-wheeling.

Grabbing the rope, we fastened it around the tree near where it made contact with the bank on the downhill side of the road. The end of the tree stuck out over the bank where it had snapped off. On the uphill side of the road the tree was about two metres off the ground.

Kelly jumped into the truck, which was already in four-wheel drive. I connected the other end of the rope, which had a large eye on it, to a hook on my frame. Bob, Wade and I stood above the tree and motioned for Kelly to back down the hill, pulling the log with him. As the rope began to tighten we could hear the wheels on my truck bucking and spinning intermittently as they tried to keep contact with the gravel surface. The tree never budged.

Signalling Kelly to stop and ease off the tension, we took a look to find out why the tree would not move. Upon close inspection, we could see that exactly where the tree made contact with the ground, it was wedged between two huge rocks buried into the road surface. We had to somehow find a way to get the tree up and over the rocks that held it fast. Looking around for some kind of lever with which to pry under the tree, I spotted a large broken limb about three metres long. Placing the limb under the tree just above where we had the rope tied, I again signalled for Kelly to start pulling the tree. Bob and Wade were still standing behind me on the uphill side.

Kelly was now getting some fairly good tension on the tree. It moved a little, and as I pried up with the limb as hard as I could, the tree began to slide up over the rock. It was going to work. I pushed with all my strength and the tree began to come free of the rock—but it just kept bending. Obviously, it was still hung up on something on the bank. Nodding my head, I implored Kelly to keep pulling. The tree had moved or at least bent about a metre when suddenly the rope broke. The tree swung back like the crack of a whip, caught me under my jaw and fractured it.

I was knocked onto my back. Intense pain shot through my face. I felt nauseated and my head reeled in pain and a sort of numbness. After about a minute of mental stupor, I got back up. No one said a thing except, "Are you okay?" I said nothing but got up, found the rope and retied it with a double knot, and we reattached it to the tree.

Following the same protocol we'd just tried, I again positioned myself with my lever and stubbornly tried again. There was no point asking for help with this attempt; I knew it would not be forthcoming. I recklessly thought the rope must have had a weak spot. Now I was confident it would hold securely; after all, it had pulled 2,300-kilo trucks out of ditches.

Kelly again tightened up the rope. The tree began to move as it bent over the rock. With me still signalling to Kelly to keep pulling, the tree moved a little more than the first time. Believing it was almost ready to pull free, I buried my head into my left shoulder against the limb and let out a yell. Simultaneous to my yell was the snap of the rope again, catching me square in the face. This time it lifted me off my feet and I hurtled uphill, passing Bob in midair with my feet flailing crazily. Five metres up the hill I landed hard on a boulder knocked loose by other trucks from previous trips.

At first the most pain I felt was in my tailbone, where I made contact with the boulder. Then it was replaced with the most intense pain I had ever felt, and I'd felt intense pain many times. I raised my hand to my face and felt the warm flow of my blood run over and through my fingers. My nose was badly broken, with a puncture from a broken limb of the tree. I sat there for a few minutes as the blood continued to flow freely. Kelly was in near hysterics and kept saying, "We need to get you to a doctor! Let's just forget about the hunt and go home!" But Bob had just driven all the way from Campbell River to our home just for the hunt and I did not want to let him down.

Getting to my feet, I staggered to the truck and told everyone we would go down to Crooked Lake and soak my face in the cold water, hoping that would stop the bleeding. Kelly backed the truck down to the pullout at the bottom and wheeled it the short distance back to the lake. I washed and soaked my face in the cold mountain lake until the bleeding stopped. Bob handed me two extra-strength Tylenol. I asked if he had more. He replied, "About half a bottle." I asked for two more, took the four pills, waited for ten minutes, then took two more.

The pain had subsided a little and with the sky starting to show signs that it would soon be dawn, I told everyone to get back in the truck. We headed over to Crooked Lake Resort, where everyone was still fast asleep. We saw the woodshed and an axe sitting in the chopping block, so we borrowed the axe and went back up the mountain road. We chopped furiously at the tree until we were finally able to pull enough of it aside by hand to allow us to drive by. No sooner had we travelled around a corner than we were met with four more trees of similar size, blown down across the road.

In shock, we never said much, just grabbed our packs and rifles, locked the truck, hid the keys along the roadside and started the eleven-kilometre hike up and in to our camp. I couldn't breathe through my nose as it was completely swollen shut, and even opening my mouth more than a slit was too painful to my jaw. Five hours later we arrived at the spot where we would pitch camp. I took the last of Bob's Tylenol then slept until just before nightfall. I could not eat yet, as my jaw pain was still equalling what I felt in my nose, if not my whole head. I slept fitfully through the night, breathing with difficulty.

I had finally fallen asleep only to be awoken seemingly moments later to the rustling of Bob and my sons getting ready to go out for the morning hunt. I opened the tent flap looking like hell warmed over, according to Kelly. He basically told me I needed to stay in camp and rest; they would be back around lunchtime. I agreed without hesitation. They said so long and began the last hike up to the alpine to hunt. I lay back in my tent and slept.

I awoke a few hours later to find that the guys had not returned yet. I reached up to touch my nose, feeling that some of the swelling had subsided. I could also feel that it was bent sharply off to the right. As a competitive boxer, I normally would not have much of an issue with that. I have been punched in the face many times—this was not a major setback. However, as vain as I am about my limited good looks, I could not afford that facial anomaly. I grabbed my nose firmly between my thumb and forefinger, took another laboured breath through my mouth, then pulled it straight. It was painful, but not nearly as much as when it got bent in the first place.

Well, we went on to have a good, successful hunt. Bob and I both got exceptional four-point muleys and, on the return, it was basically all downhill with loaded packs.

My stubbornness has been a great help to me in overcoming some difficult challenges, but sometimes it can also be my downfall. I've gotten myself into many jackpots and difficult situations, and I've had a few trips to Emergency at my local hospital, and even in the US, because of too much courage and not enough caution. But I have made promises to Ingrid and our children that I will not rush in anymore, but remember to think before I leap!

Miracle Baby

November 20, 1998, will stand out in my life—and indeed, our family's life—as one of the most frightening and miraculous experiences we have ever faced.

Ingrid and I had purchased an 835-square-metre log lodge in Anglemont, a community that borders Shuswap Lake. Well known to folks from all over the world, and especially to the neighbouring Albertans who inundate the area every summer for two solid months of fun in the sun, the Shuswap is a beautiful part of BC. With houseboating, water sports of all kinds and fifteen hundred kilometres of shoreline to explore, the lake has something for everyone.

We hoped to get our business up and running quickly. We had purchased the lodge in May of that year and started immediately upgrading it with repairs and renovations. Ingrid had been pregnant for a few months, but of course I put her to work full tilt as usual, which she took on with no complaint. Before long we had most of the renos completed, with brandnew bedding for the twenty-one bedrooms, including expensive duvets—that was Ingrid's call.

Soon we started to get bookings for our newly named Anglemont Bed & Breakfast. We still had our eighty-three-hectare ranch in Kamloops, on which we had built our new home only one year earlier, but my gypsy nature and Ingrid's desire to try doing a B&B had brought us to the purchase of this new venture. Not wanting to rent our new house out, it sat empty.

By this time we also had our thirty-two hectares of ocean-front property in Smith Inlet—to be more specific, Mill-brook Cove—with just over two kilometres of shoreline and a stream that ran through to the ocean at one of the three bays along the shoreline. I had tried mightily to persuade Ingrid to let me build a lodge there from the twelve thousand cubic metres of old growth cedar on site, which had always been my plan. Unfortunately, it was not going to happen: Ingrid was not going to take our young family to a semi-remote paradise, no matter how beautiful.

Failing that, Anglemont became the new alternative. Prior to purchasing the lodge, I had entered into an agreement to sell our waterfront property to a friend and former business associate named Rick. He was to complete the deal on July 2 of that year. I felt that with the sale of the oceanfront property and what money still remained from my logging, we would be able to promote our lodge at trade shows around the world and not need to make a significant income in-between.

On June 27, I received a call from Rick. I had that gut feeling that it wasn't good news and my instincts were spot on, as Rick informed me that his accountant said the purchase couldn't happen at this time, and he couldn't even commit to a possible completion date. I hung up the phone, shocked and disappointed. It seemed like things were conspiring against us. Not to mention that a large forest fire was now raging near Salmon Arm, and the Trans-Canada Highway was closed to traffic from Alberta for safety reasons. Smoke filled the sky southwest of us and created a bleak skyscape, although we suffered few effects from the smoke and ash that filled the sky across the lake.

Bookings were cancelled, however. We sat empty that summer, other than for our first and only Ricketts Family Reunion (which was basically a disaster, but that is another story). We hung on through the summer and were still able to enjoy the lake. Approaching Labour Day weekend, we'd had only a handful of bookings and money was becoming a large issue. We really tried to make the best of it, though, and still enjoyed our time there. We decorated the biggest Christmas tree we'd ever had that December, one a full four and a half metres high that the kids and I found in the mountains near us.

This story, so far, may seem to have little to do with a miracle; however, its purpose is to lend context and understanding to what is really most precious in life. We were doing okay, by the standards the world would use, even with the current struggles at the lodge and the sale of Millbrook Cove collapsing. An eighty-hectare ranch, thirty-two hectares of oceanfront property with $1.5 million worth of timber, and of course a gorgeous 835-square-metre log lodge. All with total mortgages of less than what a quaint house in Langley would have cost in the 1990s.

Life was still good: good marriage, good health and we were happy.

This greatest gift I refer to is one we received just over a month before Christmas. Ingrid began labour in the mid-morning of November 20 with our eighth child. By late afternoon the contractions were intense and coming in quicker and stronger increments. It was time to drive the hour and a quarter to Salmon Arm and the hospital. We loaded Ingrid's hospital bag into the truck and let the kids know it was time to go.

At the hospital, Ingrid was brought to the birthing room, where we patiently waited for the blessed event of our child. Everything seemed to go as was expected. Ingrid's contractions became even stronger and her urge to push was fully engaged. Her labours had been predictable over the years: intense back labour but usually not long once the first okay to push was given.

Ingrid pushed, holding my hand with a vice-like grip. Suddenly, we could see the head of our baby. A few more pushes and a beautiful baby girl entered our world in all her splendour.

But Dr. Grieve immediately placed our baby into an incubator behind Ingrid's bed. She looked nervous and concerned, as did the nurses in attendance. Ingrid and I were confused about why they had not passed our little girl to lie on Ingrid's breast, as was common practice with all the other children we'd had. There was muffled but concerned conversation between Dr. Grieve and the nurses.

Bringing a phone into the delivery room, Dr. Grieve spoke to a pediatric specialist at Royal Inland Hospital in Kamloops. I could hear the conversation and now understood why Ingrid had not been handed our baby. As I studied her closely, I noticed our baby girl appeared lifeless and her complexion was black. She was not breathing, nor had she been since she was delivered. As Dr. Grieve anxiously talked to the specialist on the phone, I could sense desperation and even acceptance that this baby was not going to ever breathe again.

I was stunned and in shock. Ingrid asked to see her baby but the doctor gave no response, and I could do nothing.

Then, prompted by what I know to be the Holy Spirit, I was given a message to lay my hands upon this lifeless child and pronounce a priesthood blessing upon her. I told Dr. Grieve I wanted to give our baby a blessing. She looked surprised but backed away from the incubator, as did the nurses. I laid my hands on her little head and pleaded that our Heavenly Father would give our baby back to us, by the power of the holy priesthood and in the name of Jesus Christ.

I lifted my hands from her perfect head and only moments later she took her first breath. The colour began to come into her skin, her breathing became stronger and she began to cry and move her little body. My heart was as full that day as it ever could be. I will never be able to be grateful enough to my loving Heavenly Father and my saviour, Jesus Christ, who that day gave our Kathrin Ingrid (Katie Boomer) back to us and allowed us the wonderful experiences and memories she has brought us over the years. Katie has been a tower of strength for me, and has blessed us with her sweet spirit and calming influence in a sometimes hectic and demanding world. She is special in every way.

That day, all the treasures and possessions that I thought gave me happiness paled in comparison to the special gift that was given to Ingrid and me and our family. Yes, it was an eventful and tumultuous year, but it was the most joyous Christmas we have ever had.

Random Act

You hear a lot these days about random acts of kindness being carried out—on the news, in print, on television as well as through every social media outlet. They are all great stories to hear, especially considering the onslaught of negativity that normally pervades these mediums. However, there are many random acts of kindness that go unannounced, unheralded and without any fanfare; just quiet, anonymous shows of charity, kindness and consideration for no other reason than that.

In early 2012, our family had been enjoying four weeks of road-trip holidaying through the US. Our primary purpose was to record my third album, *I Must Be Crazy*, in Nashville. After playing at the Canadian Country Music Awards in 1996, getting some radio attention, and having aired videos on CMT, I thought the Nashville sound would maybe push me up to a higher level of monetary success.

After we finished recording the album we continued driving through the southern US, crossing over from Arizona into Utah and heading into Bryce Canyon. Being April, there was not much happening, at least tourist-wise, as the official tourist season was still at least a month away. Which was perfect—I don't like crowds anyway.

We found a quiet place to stay at Bryce Canyon Resort. We may have been the only ones there. We settled in and took a little rest from our travelling, wandering about to stretch our legs. Two of our children, Jacob and Kathrin, were with Ingrid and me, and we were getting hungry so we decided to go back up the highway to a small restaurant called Foster's.

As we entered, we were met by a lovely lady who smiled warmly, escorted us to our seat and handed us the menus. We were surprised to see that a simple hamburger was over $8 US! When you're used to McDonald's burgers for under $2, $8 seems pretty high. I looked at Ingrid and quietly commented, "They want eight dollars for a hamburger?" In a few minutes this nice gal came over to take our orders. I mentioned that we would have to pass, thanked her anyway and away we went.

We had been accustomed to having entire meals, including buffets, that were under $8 so I thought we might find a better, more reasonable place to eat. After all, we were already four weeks into a six-week holiday, had recorded an album in Nashville (in fact, this was my second trip down in just over a year) and had spent a king's ransom already. Okay, I am a cheapskate but I like to think I am just frugal.

We drove into the little town of Bryce and found no place to eat. Grudgingly, we decided to go back to Foster's, bite the bullet and buy the high-priced burgers. A half-hour later, we walked back in, met the same sweet lady, got seated and ordered our hamburgers. When they arrived, I was surprised at how big and delicious they were. With the accompanying fixings it was well worth the $8+ we were charged. I motioned to the nice server—her name was Carolyn—that we were ready for our bill.

Carolyn came over to our table, smiled at us and informed me that there was no charge. I looked at her in disbelief and asked why. Without batting an eye, she simply answered that she had told the cook that if we returned the meal was on her. I was floored by this kindness and generosity, shown by a complete stranger to our family.

Still in disbelief, we thanked Carolyn profusely. Before we left she said that we should stop at the Arby's in Panguitch, where she also worked, on our way out from Bryce Canyon tomorrow. We thanked her again, although I think a mere thanks was not nearly adequate, then or now, really. We said goodbye and left. The very next day we did stop in at Arby's to have lunch and visit for a few moments with Carolyn before we headed on.

Carolyn will always have a place in our hearts, and especially mine. We stayed in touch through social media and have developed a strong connection over the past years. She has added greatly to my life and is someone I now call a dear friend. In this busy, self-absorbed world, Carolyn is a breath of fresh air and an incredible human being. I love this woman and her fine example of Christ-like love and charity, and I always will.

Hobbles and Horses

As anyone who has had horses can tell you, they can sometimes be a real handful, even the good ones. They can get you high up into the alpine after mountain goats, mule deer and grizzly bear. However, they can also leave you there all by your lonesome with an incredibly long walk back.

Let's take a couple of examples that could have very well ended up that way. My good friend Leo and I had planned an early-season mule deer hunt up in the Boss/Deception Mountain area, more specifically called Eureka Peak, a place where I love to hunt. It was on the last hot day in August. We were heading in by horseback with my Arab/Walker gelding, Dio, and my young quarter-horse mare, Diamond—this would be her first hunting trip.

Arriving at the little basin lake that was camp for the next few days, we pitched our tent, hobbled Dio (knowing Diamond would not leave Dio's side) and decided to take an afternoon siesta in the warm summer air. I lay in the tent while Leo spread out on the alpine grass. I was gently serenaded to sleep by the sound of the hobbles on Dio's feet jingling a short distance behind the tent.

I awoke with a start, not sure why, but I had a feeling that something was wrong. I first thought of grizzly bears—there were many in that area at the time. I sat up and strained to hear anything that might explain my sudden awakening. Suddenly what I was listening for, or rather what I couldn't hear, brought me to my senses. I heard no jingling of hobbles. With only my socks on, I quickly opened the tent flap and looked behind the tent. No horses.

I looked by the lake but saw nothing. Then, turning back to where I had hobbled Dio, I saw what I feared most. No, it wasn't grizzly bears. It was the sight of Dio and Diamond over three hundred metres away, with Dio hop-footing like a pro up the last hill before they would begin the six-hundred-metre descent back to the horse trailer. I ran like a world-class sprinter across jagged rocks and broken shale, still in nothing but my socks. I was gaining on them, but we were going to be dangerously close to losing them if I did not catch them before the top of the hill.

I'm not sure how I accomplished it, but I managed to catch Dio's halter as he was within steps of being downhill and home free. My lungs were on fire and my right foot throbbed in intense pain where I had broken my big toe three days earlier. Running flat out on the abrasive rocks did not help. My wool socks were shredded to confetti.

Eventually, we got the horses back to camp. I shortened Dio's hobbles and picketed him to boot.

As if that wasn't enough, a near tragic accident on our return trip could have cost the lives of both Dio and Diamond. Forty-five minutes after loading the two horses into the trailer, we were bouncing back down along the Canim-Hendrix Lake Road, heading for home. We encountered a bad washboard section and were maybe going a touch faster than we should have been. As we entered the rough stretch of road, we hit two good potholes. Leo immediately braked in anticipation of more to come. I instinctively looked back at the horses in the trailer. What I saw next caused my heart to race in abject fear.

Dio and Diamond were hurtling alongside of us on the driver's side. The trailer had come free; its safety chain had snapped. Helplessly, I watched the trailer careen toward the downhill bank, Dio's head sticking out the side window. I yelled at Leo, *"Stop the truck!"* He slammed on the brakes. The trailer flew past us and over the bank it went.

Before the truck even came to a full stop, I jumped out and ran over to what I believed would be an unimaginable level of carnage, and my beloved horses dead or dying. What I did see could only be described as miraculous. The trailer had come to a stop four metres below the road surface against a large cottonwood tree. The trailer was not upside down but sat with the nose dug into the ground at the base of the tree and the wheels sitting mostly in the air. Only the front tandem axle wheels made a little contact with the small trees it had run over.

I opened the trailer doors to see two very much alive horses. Dio was lying on top of my little mare, Diamond. Neither horse was moving, just breathing hard and covered in sweat already. Leo arrived, yelling, "Are they okay? What are we going to do?"

The trailer was on a nearly forty-five-degree angle and we had two 450-kilogram horses that would not or could not get out on their own. "Go get me the rope out of the truck," I hollered at Leo. In a moment he returned with a thick piece of braided cotton rope. I slid down the trailer until I came up against my gelding. Reaching underneath his motionless body, I wound the rope around his flank in front of his back legs.

Leo held the rope tight as I climbed up to the back of the trailer. Now all I had to do was stand on the back and pull Dio out. Sounded easy in theory, but Leo could not help as I needed to lift the horse straight up and out where there was only room for one person. I prayed for strength and God's help, as I have done more than once, then pulled as hard as I could.

Dio began to slide up the floor. When his hind end was level with my feet I swung my right foot off to the side and, standing on one leg, gave one more Herculean pull. He made a kicking motion, which brought his hind legs over the edge of the trailer. With me still pulling and his weight dropping over the back, Dio flipped over backwards, landing on the brush below. Leo had to jump out of the way to keep from being flattened by the horse's fall. Grabbing Dio's halter as he stood, shaking heavily, Leo undid the rope and led the horse up the bank to the road.

I copied the same procedure with Diamond. She was frozen in fear until I wrapped the rope around her midsection. I rubbed her neck and blood-spattered forehead, where she had received a good-sized gash. She softened, nuzzling my hand as if saying to me with those big brown eyes, "Please help me." I climbed back to the same position I was in moments ago and lifted her out of the trailer. It was if she had learned from Dio what to do and the same scenario took place, with her falling free of the trailer.

We walked the horses up and down the road to help calm them while we pondered what we were going to do next. We still had three hundred kilometres to go to get home. As we walked, a 4×4 pickup came around the corner a few hundred metres down the road with two fellows in it. They pulled over without being waved down and asked if we were okay. Pointing over the bank to the nearly invisible trailer, I asked if they had a strong cable or rope that could pull our trailer back up to the road.

Turned out they did have a strong length of steel cable. I hooked the cable to the trailer and gave the go-ahead signal. As slick as a whistle, they brought that trailer back onto the road. We thanked the two good Samaritans and off they went. The trailer seemed like it was still roadworthy, but when we went to hook it back up to the truck we discovered why it had come off. The ball was still in the trailer tongue, but we had no retainer nut. Leo scoured the section of road we were on, hoping against all odds to find it. Ten minutes later I heard him shout, "Found it!" We attached the ball back onto the truck and tightened that nut so tight with a pipe wrench it would never come off again.

Now came the hard part: loading two horses into a trailer that they had just experienced a terrible ordeal in. I led Diamond over first because she was an easier loader. She took one false step, pawing at the deck of the trailer, before climbing right back in. Taking Dio's halter, I led him over. He never even paused, just walked right in. We closed the doors, did a final check and we were on our way.

Diamond had not stopped shaking since I pulled her out of the horse trailer. It was now two hours later and, while heading down Highway 24 toward Little Fort, she was shaking so hard that we could feel it in the truck cab. I began to pray for my little two-and-a-half-year-old chestnut mare, mouthing the words but not audibly—I could see Leo was uncomfortable with that. I prayed for her to be well and healthy again. I closed my prayer with an amen and asked Leo to pull over at the next wide spot. A minute later we had pulled off to the side of the road, and I ran back to check on the horses. When I stepped up on the fender and leaned in, I saw two relaxed and very calm horses. My prayer was answered, again!

* * *

A couple years later I took another friend of mine, Ron, to Eureka Peak to hunt goat and mule deer. We had Dio and Diamond with us, and stayed at our base camp as usual. We arrived again in the late afternoon, set up camp, had dinner and soon retired to be ready for the next day. Before I headed to bed and just before dark, I took our plates down to the mountain stream that drained the meltwater from the peaks and crevices of the mountains around us.

As I kneeled to wash one of the pans, there in the mud beside the creek was a huge grizzly bear track, exactly where we had crossed not five hours before. But I had no recollection of having seen it there earlier. I glanced around, cautiously looking for the unwanted company, then quickly washed the pans and settled in for the night.

During the night in the wee hours, I awoke to the sounds of Dio blowing and snorting. I grabbed my flashlight and peered out the tent flap. Through the frosty, high mountain air I could see both horses standing within three metres of the tent. That was unusual because they typically preferred to hang out near the centre of the basin where a few small trees were growing.

The blowing from Dio had stopped though, and I went back to sleep, satisfied that nothing was wrong.

I woke at 5:00 a.m. as I usually did. My biological clock was exact, as always. This would allow me about a half-hour to saddle up and get the horses ready to head out for our day's hunt. I got dressed, walked outside and shone my flashlight around. No horses. I figured they must be lying down. I called quietly to Dio, who would normally come easily when called; still no horses yet. I continued to look until I had checked the whole basin.

Returning to the tent, I informed Ron that I thought the horses had taken off and I was going to look for them. I headed back to the trail we had come in on and crossed the creek in the moonless pre-dawn morning before I remembered the grizzly tracks I'd seen in our own tracks when washing the pans from supper the night before. I continued my search, listening for any sounds, horse or otherwise. To make it that much more intense, I'd left my 7mm Mag back in the tent. After all, I had only been going to saddle the horses. Now I was on a razor's-edge alert.

Luckily, I soon found their tracks. They had left the trail for some reason, maybe planning to take a more direct route. I never expected it was going to be a difficult task to find them, but the hobbles had broken off Dio's feet early in their escape. Fifteen minutes later, I heard some branches breaking under a heavy foot. I peered with just a little fear in the direction of the noise, and thankfully, the beast that stood fifteen metres away was my Arab/Walker, Dio. Soon I had him in hand with Diamond following close behind. The picket would thereafter be my method of choice. The hobbles just seemed like a challenge to Dio.

Yes, like I said earlier, horses are wonderful at getting you in to remote and distant places. However, you must always remember that they can leave you there too!

Just Fall

For as long as I have been hunting game and wandering the mountains and valleys of British Columbia, I have had on my hunting bucket list the denizen of high and wild places: the Rocky Mountain goat. The opportunity to hunt for one of these fine animals was a difficult challenge due to their extremely inaccessible environment, the low odds of obtaining a coveted Limited Entry Hunt (LEH) authorization and the cost. Mountain goat hunting, much like hunting mountain sheep, also requires a fairly decent level of conditioning. You don't need to be an elite athlete, but couch potatoes might find it just a tad too taxing.

Eureka Peak and Boss/Deception Mountain was an area I had hunted before for some exceptional mule deer bucks. We had also seen some nice mature goats, and some of the billies displayed good horns. Returning from a very successful muley hunt, I anxiously awaited the next hunting season's LEH applications becoming available, in hopes of applying for one of those vaunted authorizations. The following May the LEH applications were out. I wasted no time in opening the pages that would cover the Eureka Peak area, where I hoped to be fortunate enough to hunt.

I found the appropriate page and looked for the draw area to see the number of tags to be given out and the odds. I almost fell off my chair. With childlike excitement, I saw that there were seven authorizations, which was not nearly as important as what the stated odds would be. After all, it was like winning a lottery, where some draws had odds of 250 to one. My eyes grew big and my heart raced. There before my eyes were the odds I would face: one to one!

That same day I mailed in my application. Seven weeks later I received an envelope from the government. Ripping it open, I let out my Métis war whoop. There it was: I was authorized to harvest one goat from the Eureka Peak area! Only a few short weeks later, on August 31, I was preparing to leave with my son Wade and two hunting companions. The season for both mule deer bucks and LEH goats would open on September 1. We loaded my 1959 Chev Apache stock truck and trailer with my gelding, Dio, and two quarter horse mares, Ebony (my big black) and Goldie, a less than energetic palomino.

We left our beautiful ranch in Lone Butte, where we were still living at the time, first thing in the morning, when we knew the grocery store would be open. Ebony and Goldie probably looked back at the barn and pasture with sadness, as they never liked having to work too hard, but Dio was full of piss and vinegar, ready to climb mountains and as anxious as we were to be climbing up and onto Eureka Peak and the surrounding alpine bordering Tweedsmuir Park on the western edge. Stopping in 100 Mile House, just a short drive north, we picked up the last few supplies we needed and were back on our way. Bob and Keith followed in Bob's little Chev Tracker.

Three hours later we arrived at Crooked Lake, rested for a little while, then drove the last two kilometres to a pull-off about thirty metres from the main gravel road, where we would offload the horses and gear. The road would continue on its way, eventually coming out to Horsefly, a small logging and ranching community that was aptly named.

All of my horses were pack and saddle trained. We would ride and walk intermittently, with one of the group walking in shifts. We wore large, heavy backpacks while we rode and the person walking would take a lighter pack. I usually preferred to have only one companion on this kind of hunt, as one horse could then be used solely for packing.

Nevertheless, with everyone loaded, final checks complete and the truck keys stored away in the bush nearby, we were on our way. We would make a seven-hundred-metre climb in elevation, and the trip into base camp would take four to five hours. The trip up was without any incident. The weather was fair and still relatively warm, which was expected considering it was only the last day of August. We did see one large covey of blue grouse on the trip.

Early afternoon found us at our base camp. Our tents were pitched and the horses were unsaddled. We had a little free time before I would hobble Dio until the next time the horses would be needed. Just like Diamond, Ebony and Goldie were content just to hang with Dio—as long as Dio was contained, so were the mares.

We spent a lazy afternoon gathering a few bits of firewood from the surrounding bush and enjoying a nice meal of moose stew. My sweetheart Ingrid had dehydrated the meal a few days earlier to keep the weight to a minimum.

We woke at 4:30 the next morning and after a couple of Ingrid's homemade sportsman bars (like Eat-Mores) we left on shank's mare, as they say—on foot. We walked up the steep face that towered above the basin we would call home for the next six or seven days. Even though the mornings at twenty-three hundred metres were frosty and cool, the temperatures could possibly climb to the low teens. Depending upon our success we might have to leave sooner than the allotted time, which was fine with us because that would mean we were successful.

Thirty minutes later, we had reached the top of the rock face and climbed onto the hog's-back ridge that would carry on upward at a relatively easy slope until it reached the top of Eureka Peak two kilometres in the distance. We were in beautiful alpine. Small determined juniper-like bushes tenaciously held to the thin layer of soil, and pockets of alpine flowers were now feeling the effects of the oncoming fall, starting to die and lose their springtime brilliance. Winter weather was only a few short weeks away and could soon cover the mountains in a deep blanket of snow.

The first day we were surprised to see no muley bucks that presented a reasonable shot. Carrying on up until we were within sixty metres of Eureka's peak, I spotted a billy going over the hog's-back ridge just a short distance in front of us. I rushed to the edge he had fled over, looked down and saw nothing. How could that be? He was just there moments ago.

The nearly sheer face on the north side of Eureka was fairly open with no visible place to hide, as far as I could tell. I continued to glass then suddenly, like a ghost appearing from nowhere, I saw this same billy, only now he was two hundred metres away and about seventy metres lower on the mountainside than I was.

He came out onto a flat ledge about three metres wide and shaped like an oval. Perfect, I thought. If I could drop him where he stood he would have no chance of falling the almost five hundred metres before coming to an abrupt stop beside Flathead Lake, which was nestled in the forest floor below. If that were to happen it would leave me with nothing but bones and hide. The nice horns it had grown would be in pieces and there would be little or no meat to salvage.

Finding a good rest for my 7mm Mag, I laid my small day pack down as a cushion, took careful aim and squeezed off my 150-grain Nosler on its way to the mark. Bob, watching from behind with his binoculars, assured me of a perfect spine shot as the goat instantly dropped. I kept my scope fixed on the lifeless trophy to be sure that I had just successfully harvested my first ever Rocky Mountain goat.

The joy of that moment was snatched from me when the billy began to rise from the dead, slowly coming to its feet. I was in disbelief and unwilling to shoot again, afraid if I hit him it would be enough impetus to knock him off the ledge as he was now within a metre of the drop-off. Still hoping I had him, I waited for him to collapse where he stood. As if on some vengeful prompting, he took a sideways step toward the edge then fell for the last time, 375 metres below! As he fell so did my hopes that, even if I could get to him, there would be anything left to retrieve.

Then the realization came that regardless, by law I had to bring the jaw for inspection at the local conservation office.

Looking for the safest means to get to where my goat had fallen, I realized I would have to cover some awfully scary terrain. The only viable option was to go alongside the mountain face and slowly drop my elevation until I came to the ledge where he had stood. The first 150 metres were not too difficult to navigate as a small goat trail was already etched into the mountainside.

The pace slowed considerably from there on. Nearing the last fifty metres or so, I was met by a sheer, wet face of granite nearly ten metres wide. Water was running down from the last snow that had hung on from the previous winter. I saw no other alternative than to cross this obstacle. Once I had, I would have only a short distance to get to the ledge, which was still about three metres below me.

If I could run fast enough and maintain a slight downward angle, I felt I would have enough momentum to come out level with the ledge and cross successfully. If I was too low, I would run out of mountain and continue on over the edge myself, to join my billy on the jagged, boulder-strewn moraine below.

I said a silent prayer and launched myself across the slippery slope. Running like a cartoon figure with fast feet but not gaining much speed, I was fortunate to leap the required distance to reach my mark. After taking a brief and grateful rest, I carefully walked to the ledge and peered down. I could not see my goat clearly but I could see the blood-spattered rocks below, signifying exactly the course he had fallen along. Now the question was, how was I going to get down to where he had come to rest?

Certainly, following the same path was out of the question. It was a nearly sheer drop for thirty-five metres, then a series of tiny outcroppings that would offer little help to an inexperienced mountain climber like me. Skirting along the nearly perpendicular side of the mountain, I was able to find little chimneys that would descend a short distance before ending, but there was always another outcropping that would allow me to continue my descent.

After one and a half hours of tense, difficult effort, I found myself looking at the badly beaten corpse of what should have been a milestone and an accomplished moment in my life. Instead it was a regretful sight to witness, not because I had killed a beautiful wild Rocky Mountain goat but because there was nothing really salvageable except the horns, which were miraculously the only things that seemed relatively intact. There was just a small chip on the right horn near the tip.

I sat for a few minutes and reflected on the past couple of hours that had brought me to this point. What was to have been a joyous victory was now swallowed up in remorse and anger that I had not fired one more shot into him before he took those last faltering steps, which had brought me to this point. I snapped myself back to reality and the task now at hand: to remove the skull, which was required for inspection on my return to 100 Mile House.

Loading the skull into my day pack, I began my ascent back to the top where, undoubtedly, Wade, Keith and Bob would be impatiently waiting. The first 150 or so metres, I made good time. There were plenty of large rocks and small outcroppings to climb through and get good footholds and handholds on. At that point the mountain became much steeper as the moraine began to disappear below me.

Soon my progress slowed considerably because of my fatigue, the steepness of my ascent and now a fierce thirst I couldn't quench. I'd left my water back up at the spot I took my original shot from and was now finding that the fear and anxiety I had felt over the past few hours had given me a bad case of cotton mouth. Having no water to quench my parched throat only exacerbated the situation.

I continued trying to find crevices and small chimneys that I could use to gain some altitude. I had now covered more than half the distance back to the top of the ridge from which I'd first spotted the goat. I had been climbing, including the descent, for nearly three hours. My arms were beginning to feel the effects of dehydration and the difficult climb I had so far completed. The near-vertical climb that I yet had to attempt, or rather that I needed to accomplish, would be taking its toll too. But there was, in my opinion, no other option.

Another hour of arduous hand-over-hand climbing ensued as I constantly sought out toeholds that I could jam the toe of my boots into to help give my tired arms some support and respite.

I was now, I guessed, within only about sixty metres of the summit. I was still unable to see the top of the ridge, as the going, at least at this point, was perpendicular with few handholds. I had come to a Mexican standoff: unwilling to give up the much-needed distance I had just so laboriously climbed, but unable to find a suitable route the rest of the way up. Straight up was the only way. The one consolation I had at the moment was that the place where I had come to an abrupt halt was also the only place on that sheer piece of granite that I was able to find a small remaining clump of snow. I ravenously chewed the grainy chunks and savoured every delicious swallow of cold mountain elixir. Thankfully, it gave me renewed strength and conviction.

Looking hard above me, I searched for every possible niche or fault in the rock that could be used to gain more elevation. I found a few small cuts in the face and was able to make progress, albeit little, but progress all the same. As I climbed, I had no other option but to work my way along laterally to keep finding handholds, even though they brought me back over a sheerer, more dangerous drop. I had no choice now; there was no way I would be able to retrace my steps back down. But now I was unable to see those precious little cracks in the rock that I had just climbed from. I continued until I came to a small ledge that protruded out of the mountain like the half circle of a table; it was twenty to thirty centimetres deep and close to forty centimetres wide.

I took a short breather there before searching for more cracks and openings that I could use to continue my climb. A small vertical fissure off to my left was within reach. Directly above me was a little tuft of moss. There had to be a nook or crevice there to hold enough soil to allow that moss to grow.

I reached up nearly as far as I could and thankfully was able to reach it. I dug at the moss and uncovered a good-sized cutout that would allow me to get most of my right hand snugly in. Taking another big breath and stretching out with my left hand, I could just reach the vertical fissure. I pulled myself upward. Frantically, I scratched and kicked at the rock below me, having neglected the fact that I would need something to support me as I made the next attempt for a new handhold. Finally my right foot found a spot to use as an anchor.

Working my fingers up the fissure with my left hand, I was able to get enough elevation to spot a torpedo-shaped outcrop about the size of a potato. Just above that, the ground levelled out to a good-sized ledge that would make the climbing much easier for the last fifty metres or so. With my right foot still in its little foothold, and knowing I was still about fifteen to twenty centimetres short of reaching the rock outcrop, I would have to try to jump and then grab for it.

My arms began to shake and I could feel my strength draining quickly—*now or never* came to mind. I jumped, grabbing the outcrop, and pulled myself up. But what I thought was a solid part of the mountain in reality was just a football-shaped rock jammed into the crevice that it filled, wedged in with eons worth of grit and dust. It suddenly pulled free and the rock tumbled past my head.

I frantically clawed for another grip and seemed for a moment to defy gravity while I searched—and then I fell. Mercifully, my feet caught the little ledge below me, and I landed with my face and body tight to the rock face. I hit the ledge but my momentum almost pushed me backwards over the edge.

My adrenaline was pumping hard at the realization of how close I had come to ending my life. Slowly and carefully, I turned and lowered my spent body to a sitting position on the ledge. Looking out over the beauty of the valley below and the little jewel of Flathead Lake, I was almost at peace. As I sat there, I reflected on my life and how the thirty-five years I had lived so far had been pretty full and complete (at least at thirty-five that was what I thought ...).

It had now been over four and a half hours of climbing. My arms still shook with complete exhaustion, as did my legs. At that point something began to happen to me that to this day is inexplicable. I felt content to just sit there, with no more terror of dying by falling to my death. My body was beginning to feel almost warm and comfortable.

Then another strange thing happened. I leaned forward, peering down the mountain. Sixty-five metres below me was a jumble of sharp, jagged rocks. From this vantage I could see nothing to stop my fall until I reached those rocks. Then a voice came clearly to me: "Just fall and it will all be over." The voice was pleasant and soothing.

Again I heard the same gentle admonition: "Just fall."

I slowly leaned out from the ledge that held me safe and semi-captive. But as I began to feel myself lose contact with the ledge, I heard another voice. This voice was more commanding, yet still calm: "What does your patriarchal blessing tell you?"

I stopped my forward motion and suddenly my mind became a montage of images. Truly, like a drowning person whose life flashes before their eyes in those last few moments, I too relived, in mere milliseconds, my whole life. My children and my wife, Ingrid, came into my mind vividly. Then I remembered one particular part of my blessing that said I would serve a mission with my wife and it would be glorious!

With a new resolve and a determination that filled every corner of my soul, I turned to face my enemy, and with a prayer for strength I again began to climb. I retraced my progress up the face until I reached the place that had nearly cost me my life only a short time before. There was no more rock outcropping, only a tiny ledge that I could grab with my right hand. As the fissure to my left was now mostly gone, I would have to rely on my right hand and its tenuous grip to pull my ninety-eight kilograms of body weight and clothing up onto that life-saving ledge. Letting go of the last remaining and now nearly non-existent crevice, I pulled with my right hand.

It was almost surreal as I felt my body being raised up, almost effortlessly, until I could reach with my left hand to secure another grip. I did, and moments later lay prone upon a sizable outcrop. After a brief rest I was able to ascend the remaining short distance to the ridge with little difficulty, where I found three very relieved men. When they'd heard the rocks tumbling down the mountain and my screams when I fell, they were about to consider me dead.

I feel that two forces were at work that day as I sat on that little ledge, and thank God I listened to the right voice!

Lights, Camera, Action!

Since receiving my first guitar at nine years of age, music has played a huge role in my life. It has been my trustworthy side-kick that I've taken with me almost everywhere. It was my intermediary with my family and all those I met in my life. I could say things and express my innermost feelings through my music, disguised in a song I wrote. It was also my counsellor and best friend. Particularly when I was young, my songs were often my only means of communication as I stuttered and stammered my way through the difficulties and trials I faced. I had no other way to communicate effectively without being afraid of reprisal or told to be quiet.

As I grew older, the guitar still gave me that audience I needed and was my release-and-purge outlet, my best way of expressing myself. However, as I entered my teens, I began to explore other aspects in my music, moving from just exploring my reality through music to absorbing a little more of the mainstream influence: the Beatles, Elvis Presley and other well-known artists of that era. Over the years I expanded my repertoire and eventually even submitted some of my original compositions to record labels. I received a few nice form letters but nothing really transpired.

I felt that if something was ever going to happen to get my music out to the public, I would need to be the one solely responsible. I submitted my rudimentary demos to radio stations and even a couple of television shows that were showcasing new artists. Nothing positive came from it, and I felt that maybe I just didn't have what they wanted, or I simply didn't have the talent necessary to garner any interest.

All that changed in 1980, as I was nearing my twenty-fifth birthday, when I received a call from a producer with the *Vancouver* show on what was then CKVU-TV (now Citytv). I was informed that they had enjoyed my demo of "It's Too Late" and wanted me to perform it on the show. I excitedly agreed. The producer gave me the details, including when I needed to be there to do makeup and get some pre-performance instruction.

I hung up the phone in disbelief, fear and joyful exuberance. The joyful exuberance only lasted for a few minutes, until the reality of what I was about to do set in. I practised endless hours for the next week. On the day of the show, I kissed my mom, said "Wish me luck" and left New Westminster for the studio in Vancouver, getting there around 4:00 p.m. Shaking with fear, I entered the building and cornered the first person I saw for help. The kind fellow pointed me in the right direction. I found and was introduced to the producer and was asked if I had any questions about what was about to happen. I had a million of them but instead, I said no!

I was escorted into the green room, where I would have makeup applied—no, not eyeliner and lipstick, but just some cake to take away glare and keep my sweating down to a gentle stream. As I was getting my makeup done, another group of young men came into the room, four guys who had formed a band and were going to debut on the program too. We acknowledged each other, and then it was time for me to go on. I was to be the first performer.

I was led into the studio, where a small stage was waiting with a microphone set up for my guitar and another for my vocals. The light was kept low and would stay low until it was time for my live performance. I could feel the sweat running down my back, and my hands felt like granite. Moments passed during which I heard nothing, then suddenly the floor director was doing the countdown to my performance. I swallowed hard one last time and waited for the floor director to get to one. The red light came on, indicating that we were now live, and that was my cue to start my performance. I looked at the camera directly in front of me and suddenly I could hear myself beginning to play the introduction.

As I sang the first line of "It's Too Late," it just sort of fell out of my mouth. Still trembling inside, I continued. I had just started the chorus when I noticed the cameraman moving his feet and body to the melody. He may never know how much that relaxed me from that point on. I finished my performance and received warm applause and even a few cheers. I stood up from my stool, bowed my head in thanks and was again escorted to the green room. When I entered the room, the band that was waiting their turn exclaimed that I was awesome! They were so kind.

My mother cried as she watched my performance. My family was proud of me, maybe for the first time in my life. But when I contacted my father's girlfriend, Nicky, to see what my dad thought, she informed me that he never saw it. I was confused. I had told them when it would be on as soon as I knew.

I asked, "Did it not show up for them to see?"

She replied, "I saw it, with two of our friends. You did great. But your dad did not see it." Again I asked why. Apparently Dad had told Nicky that he didn't want to be embarrassed by me or my performance!

Undaunted by the rejection I felt that day, I planned to carry on, with or without his support or pride in me. I continued performing in clubs and bars in and around Campbell River, with quite a few gigs at the Salmon Point Resort, and I performed at the Merritt Mountain Music Festival and in a showcase at the Canadian Country Music Awards in Calgary in 1996. I have since recorded three albums, won two Billboard Songwriting Awards, had top-twenty hits in Canada and Europe (cracking top ten in Europe) and made seven music videos (two for CMT). And even now, after a few years' hiatus from my guitar and writing, I'm back at it. I recently wrote a song on a political note that received over fifty thousand views on Facebook and had three thousand shares within the first month. I am happy to say that the guitar and my music hold a place in my heart and life once more.

About the Author

Kelly Randall (Zeus) Ricketts is a husband, father of nine, grandfather and great-grandfather. He is proud of his Cree-Métis heritage and is a devout member of the Church of Jesus Christ of Latter-Day Saints. Professionally, he is a singer-songwriter with three albums (two country/country rock, one R&B/country), seven music videos and two top-twenty hits (one making top ten in Europe). He is also a logger, miner, horseman/wrangler and former heavyweight boxing champion who fought in the Canadian Olympic trials for the 1988 Olympics in Seoul, Korea.

But that is not the extent of his life's work: he is an avid hunter who has worked as a fisherman, fishing guide, taxidermist, boxing coach, sawyer, builder/carpenter, welder/fabricator, mechanic, heavy-duty tireman, heavy-equipment operator, millwright and butcher, and has studied both psychology and sports administration.

Despite living half his life on various parts of Vancouver Island, Kelly has lived in almost every region of British Columbia and even spent a few unforgettable years in Saskatchewan. Kelly, Ingrid and their youngest daughter Kathrin now live off grid on thirty seven hectares of waterfront on Takysie Lake in Central British Columbia, on the south side of Francois Lake.